INTRODUCTION

Welcome to "Easy Coloring - Food and Drinks for Everyday Fun Vol.1," This large book sized at 8.5 x 11 inches, featured bigger and bolder designs perfect for those who love coloring bigger and bolder.

Inside, you'll discover a delightful collection of simple and artistic designs curated by a professional artist. Whether you're a beginner or experienced, there's something for every taste and skill level in these pages.

But that's not all! Alongside the beautiful illustrations, you'll also find an easy lesson on preventing color bleeding from your pages, ensuring that your artwork stays pristine and vibrant. Additionally, a PDF download is included, featuring extra colored references on similar subjects to spark your imagination and inspire your color choices.

But wait, there's more fun to be had! Dive deeper into the world of food and drinks with fun facts accompanying each subject.

Learn interesting tidbits while you color, adding an extra layer of enjoyment to your coloring experience.

Grab your favorite coloring tools and get ready to embark on a colorful journey filled with flavor, fun, and fantastic designs. Let the coloring adventure begin!.

COPYRIGHT

All rights reserved. No part of this book may be reproduced in any form or by any electronic or mechanical means. Including information storage and retrieval systems, without written permission from the author, except for brief quotations linking to the author and buying page.

The buyer-owner of this book has the right to photocopy samples for personal use only. .

Thank you for respecting my works as an author and wish you enjoy your tattooing with best results.

Copyright © 2024 Alex Metsovas for AlexartBooks

ISBN 9798325707650

See more of my books here :

amazon.com/author/alexartbooks

ABOUT THE AUTHOR

Welcome to the colorful world of AlexartBooks With a passion for art that spans over 45 years, I've explored a multitude of mediums and styles, from the intricate details of graphite pencil realism to the vibrant expressions of acrylic paintings and decorative designs.

Artistry for All Ages

In my coloring books, I strive to bring joy and inspiration to both kids and grown-ups alike. Unlike many others, my designs are born from a deep connection to the world of art. Each carefully curated illustration is handpicked to offer not only enjoyable coloring experiences but also a touch of artistic sophistication. **With my extensive background in various art forms, I ensure that every line, shape, and analogy contributes to a richer artistic journey for the colorist.**

Empowering Your Creativity

Beyond providing beautiful designs, I'm committed to empowering your creativity. In addition to the pages awaiting your colorful interpretations, I share valuable tips and tricks for coloring success. Whether you're a novice or seasoned artist, my goal is to enhance your skills and ignite your imagination.

Your Artistic Companion

Think of me not only as the creator of these coloring books but also as your artistic companion. Need advice or inspiration? Reach out to me through my Facebook or YouTube channel, where I offer service and guidance.

Join me on this colorful journey, where every stroke of the pencil or marker becomes a celebration of creativity and self-expression. Let's embark on an adventure together—one filled with beauty, inspiration, and endless possibilities.

Thank you for choosing AlexartBooks as your artistic guide.

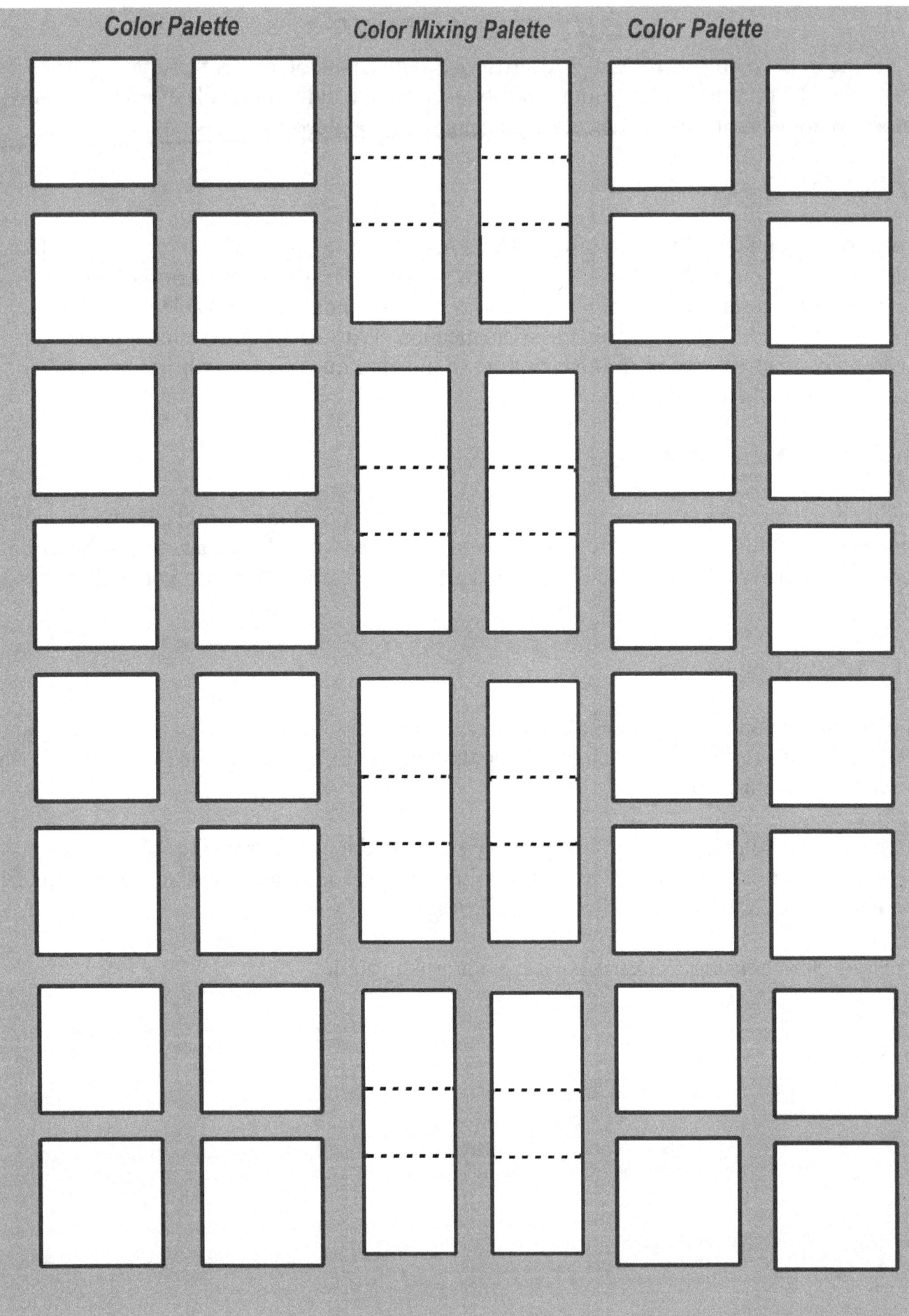

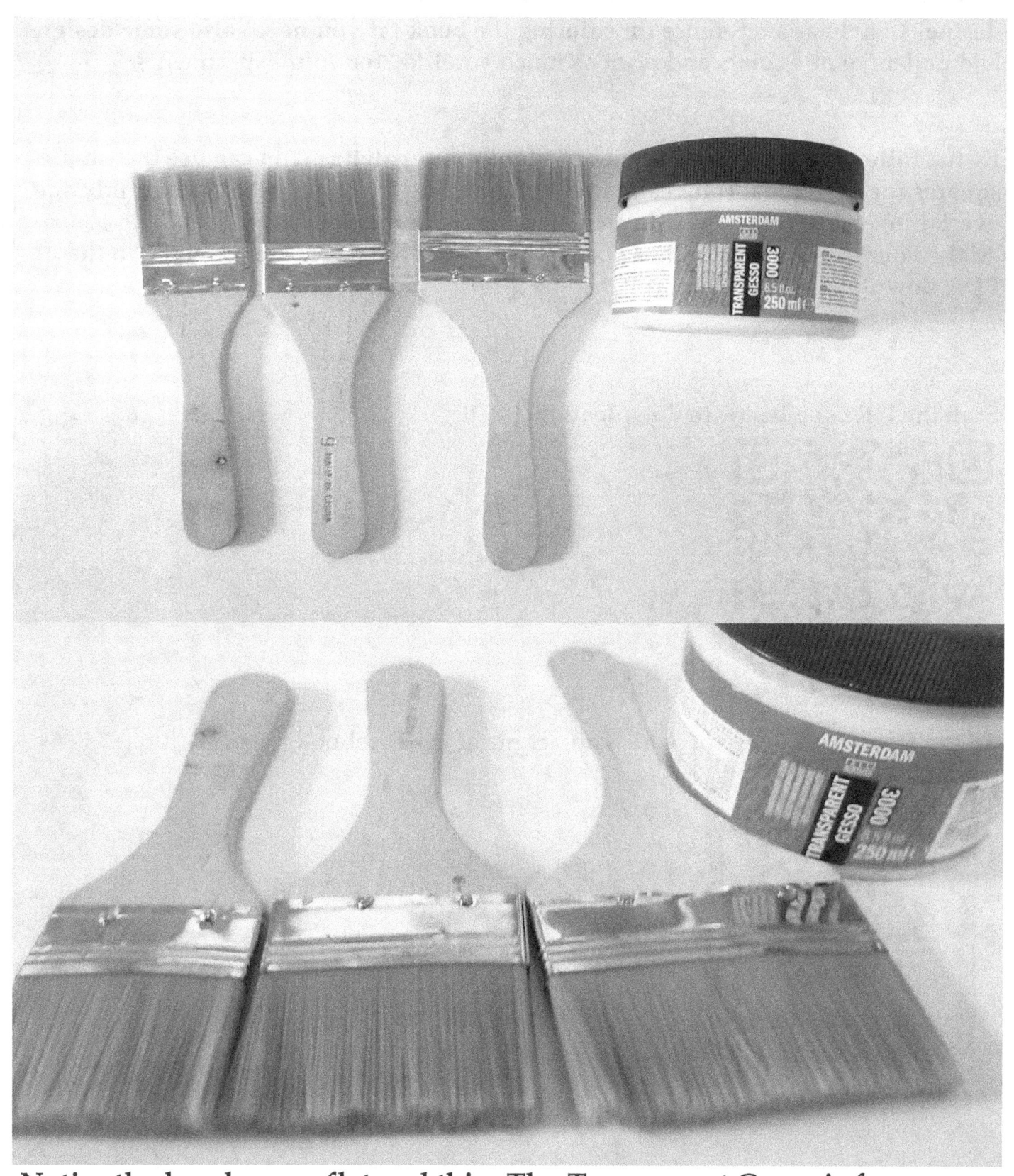

Notice the brushes are flat and thin. The <u>Transparent</u> Gesso is form Talens- Amsterdam series, but other good quality transparent Gesso from art supplies shop, will do. It just has to be transparent

PDF Download, In the PDF download you will find some colored examples of desings to help as a reference for coloring the book (if you need) also some designs and pallete to mix colors and print as much you like for your experiments.

IN the following pages are a serries of blank color palettes .You can use the single squares for individual colors and the "color mixing " row for testing color mix and overlaping colos in the "mixing area" marked with the dots.
 Make your experiments in those pages. More of these pages are provided in the PDF download so you can print

Scan the QR code below to download the PDF

IF the Download does not work contact me at my Facebook page.

HOW TO PREVENT PAGES FROM COLOR BLEEDING

Now how about making those pages resistant to color bleed of the markers ? There are 2 easy ways to do it.
  1. We have to apply <u>LIGHT coat</u> of transparent gesso. Any transparent gesso from art supplies will do

APPLICATION.
1. With a sponge brush or another light flat brush (take care to have a correct bigger size – optimal is 1-2 inch brush for that) , dip the brush to the gesso , dry it , remember we want only a little and apply to the page evently,one pass will do.

It needs very little and thin layer, let it dry for 10-15min. you may apply a second pass if necessary please experiment on a blank paper to see if it needs. Usually it does not. Make sure the book is open while it dries so the pages do not stick together..
We need a little we do not want to go aggressive to the paper and wet it too much or deform it.

You will find a video about it in my YouTube Channel. Scan the below code to go to my video or the channel and search for "
Learn how to stop color bleeding of markers and inks from coloring book pages." video demonstration. .

The first known record of donuts dates back to the early 19th century when Dutch settlers brought them to America.

The full name for a donut with a hole in the center is a "ring donut" or "torus."

The largest donut ever made weighed over 1.7 tons and was made in Utica, New York, in 1993.

The Guinness World Record for the most donuts eaten in 3 minutes without licking the lips is 29 and was achieved by Patrick Bertoletti in 2012

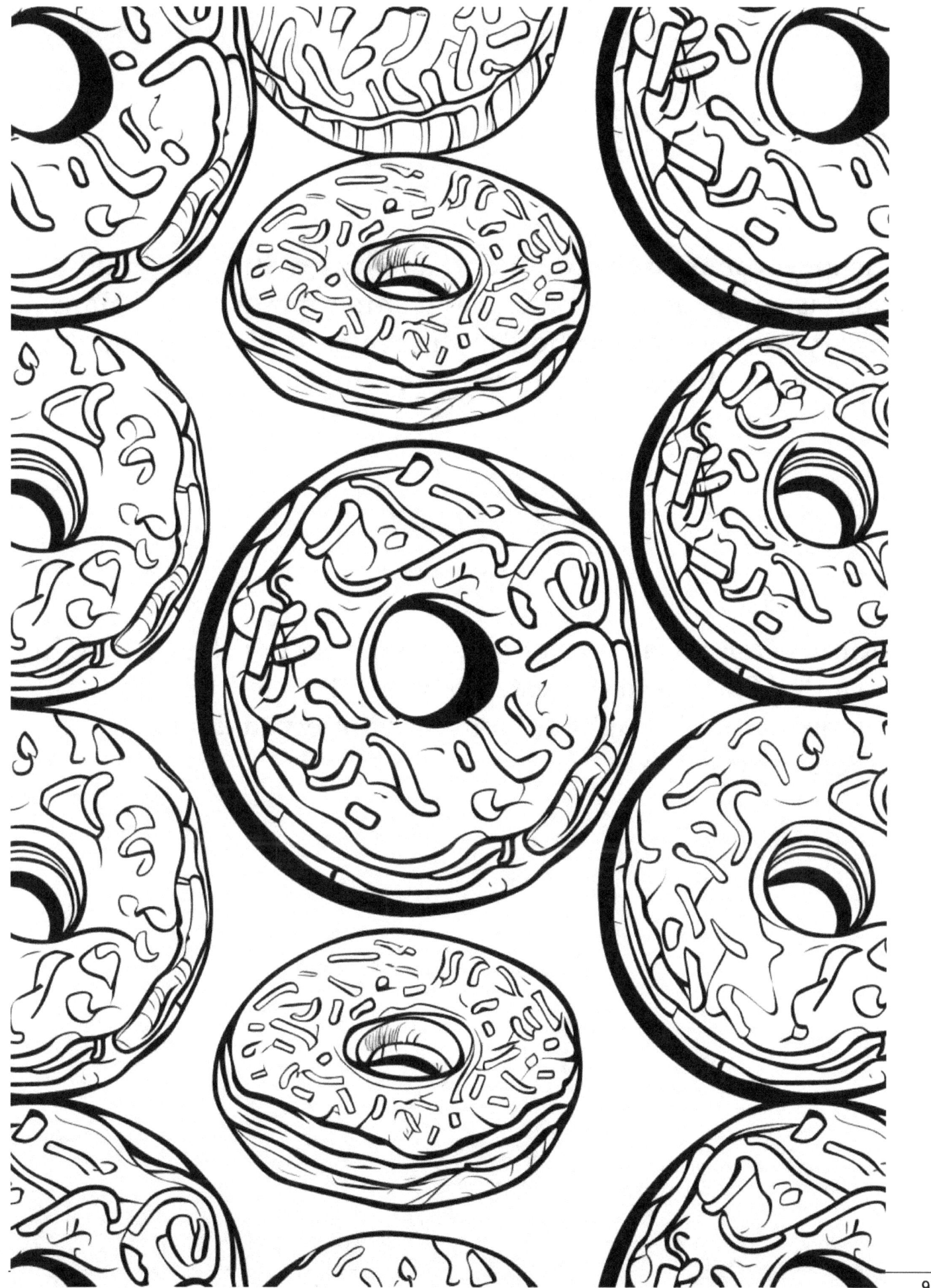

The most common shape for donuts today, with a hole in the center, is credited to a New England ship captain named Hanson Gregory, who punched a hole in the center of his fried dough to make it easier to eat while steering his ship.

National Donut Day is celebrated on the first Friday of June in the United States and was established in 1938 to honor the Salvation Army "Doughnut Lassies" who served donuts to soldiers during World War I.

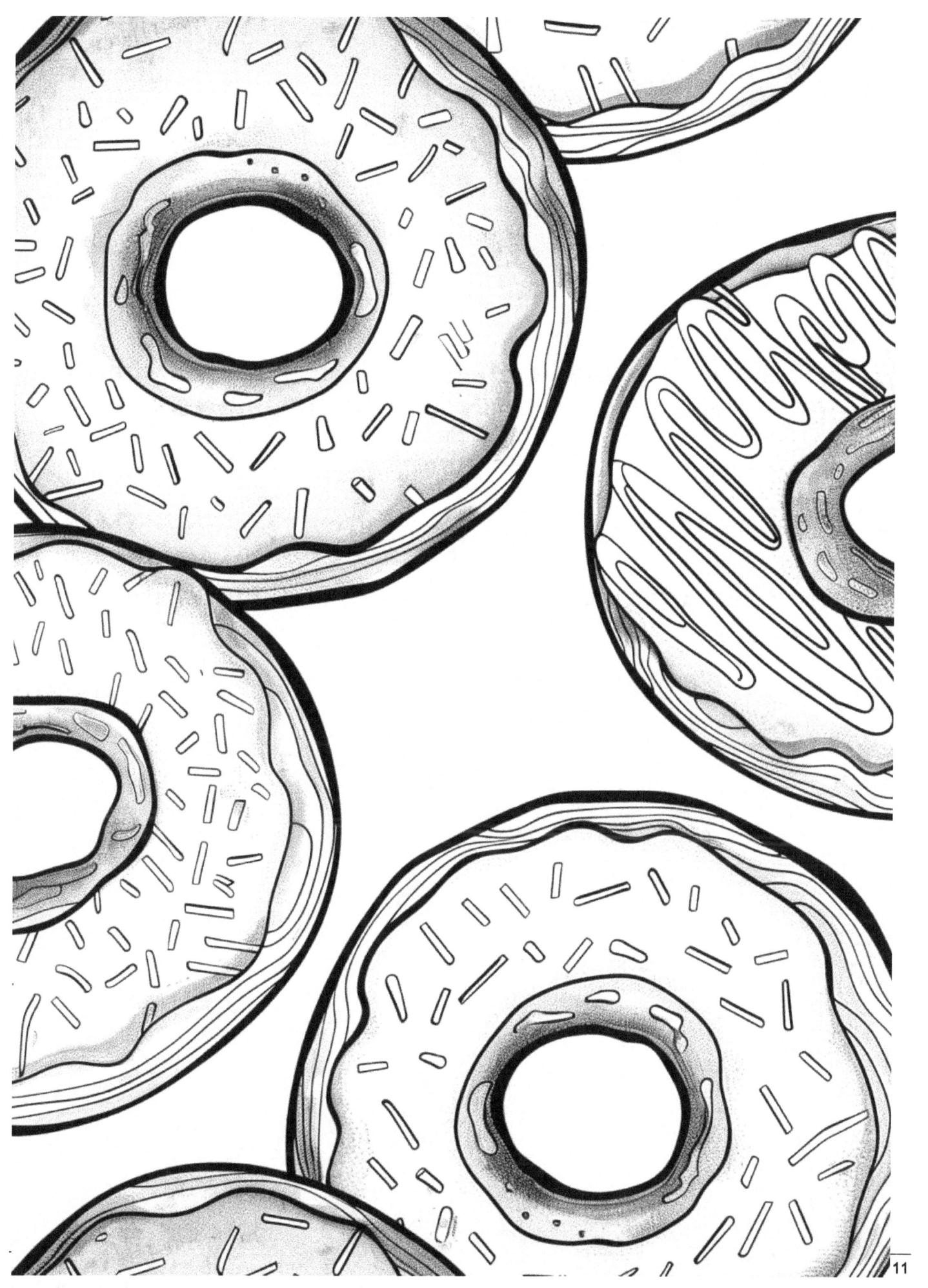

Donuts are also popular in other countries, with variations like churros in Spain, beignets in France, and loukoumades in Greece.

The word "donut" is often shortened to "doughnut," with both spellings being widely accepted.

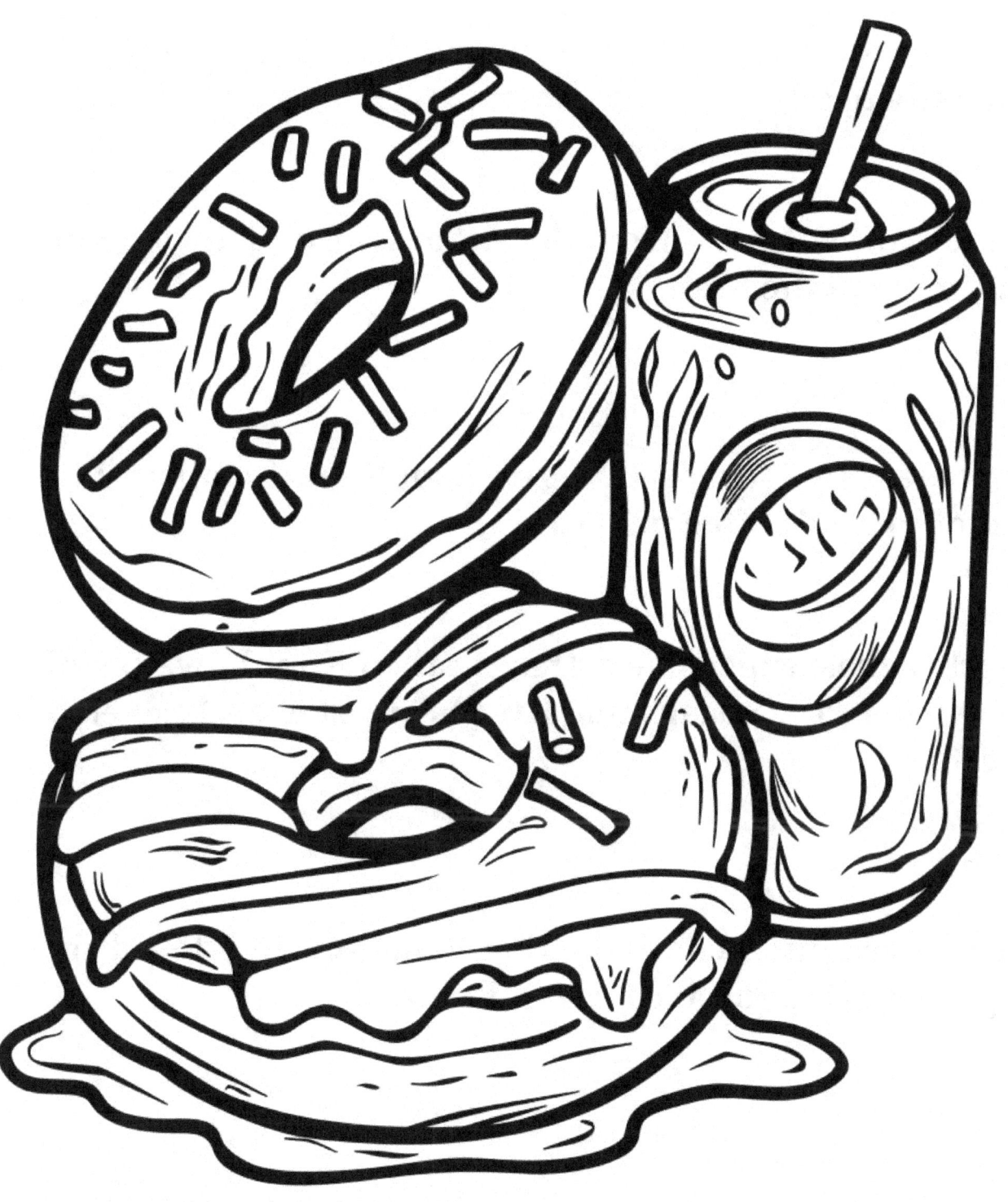

Coffee is one of the most traded commodities in the world, second only to oil.

The word "coffee" comes from the Arabic word "qahwa," which means "wine of the bean."

The average coffee tree produces enough beans for about 1 pound of roasted coffee per year.

The world's most expensive coffee is called Kopi Luwak, which is made from coffee beans that have been eaten and excreted by civet cats.

Coffee was originally chewed rather than brewed into a drink, dating back to around 1000 AD in Ethiopia.

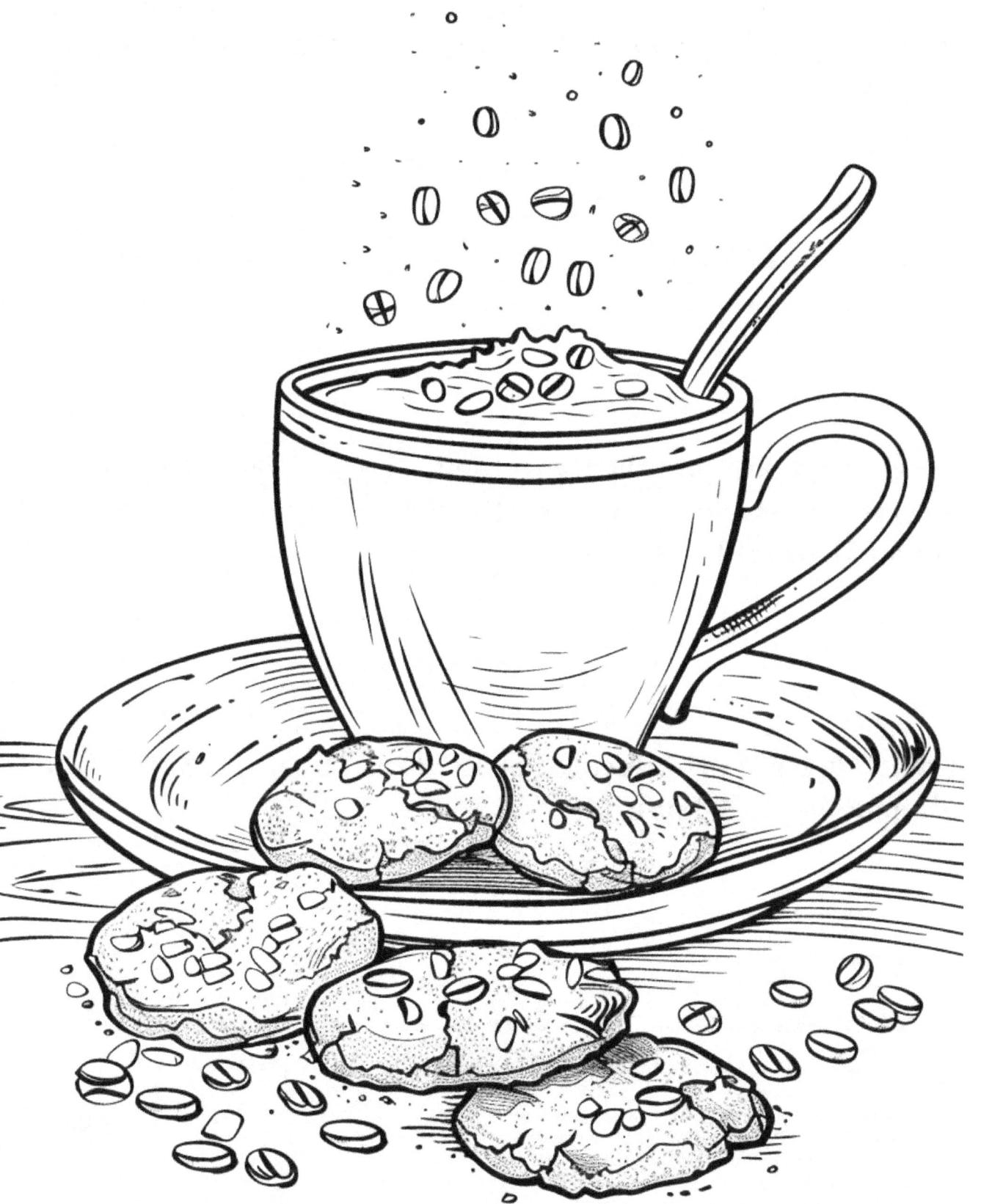

The origin of the cupcake can be traced back to the late 18th century, when they were called "number cakes" and baked in small cups.

The term "cupcake" first appeared in a cookbook in 1828.

Cupcakes gained popularity in the United States during the 19th century, especially during the Great Depression when they were an affordable treat.

The Guinness World Record for the largest cupcake ever made weighed over 1,200 pounds!

Cupcakes come in countless flavors and decorations, making them a favorite dessert for parties and celebrations.

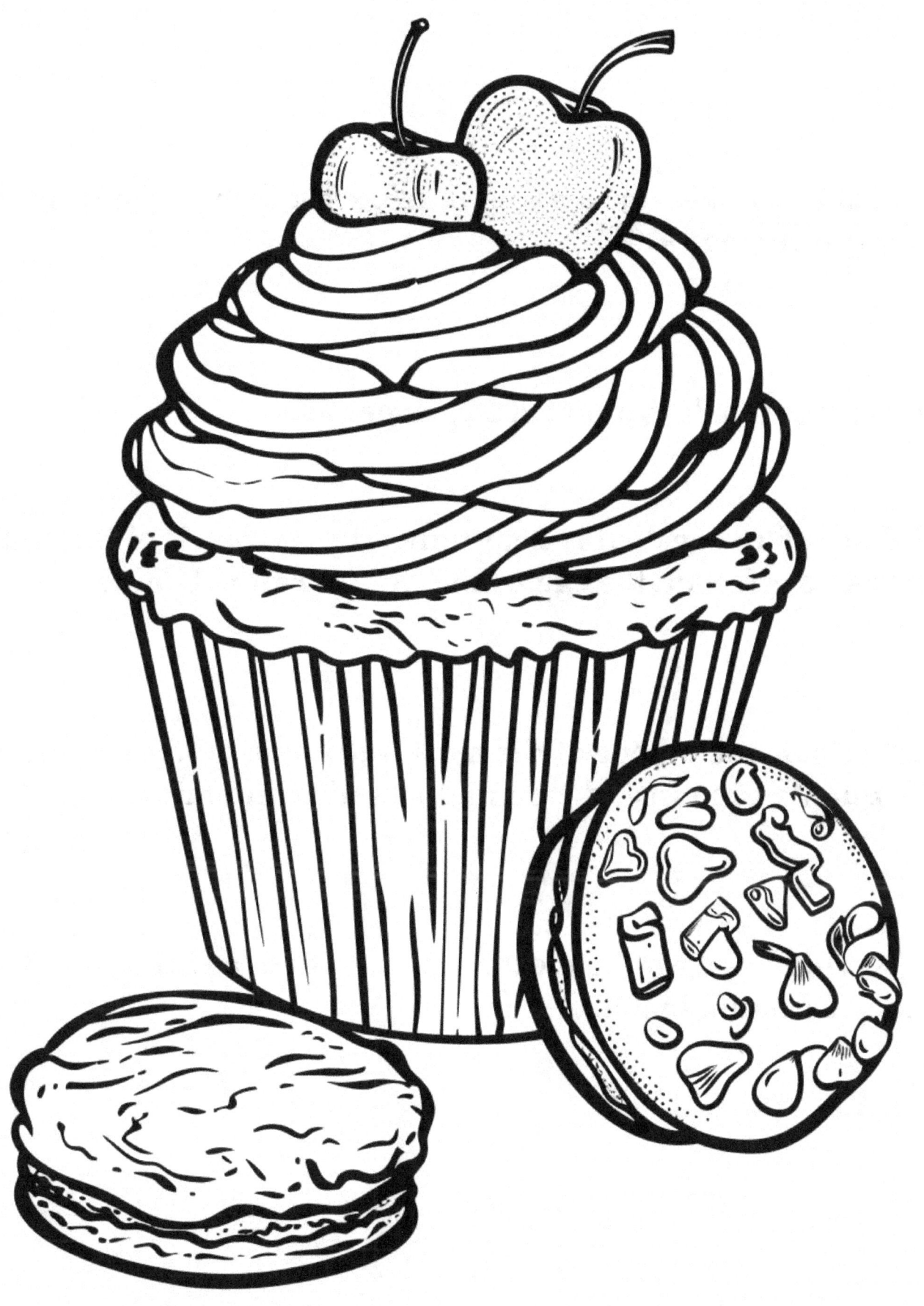

Bacon and eggs became a popular breakfast dish in the United States during the 1920s.

The average hen lays about 300 eggs per year.

The color of an eggshell is determined by the breed of the hen and has no effect on the egg's flavor or nutritional value.

Eggs are considered one of the most nutritious foods, containing high-quality protein and essential vitamins and minerals.

The world record for the most eggs eaten in one sitting is 141, set by Joey Chestnut in 2013.

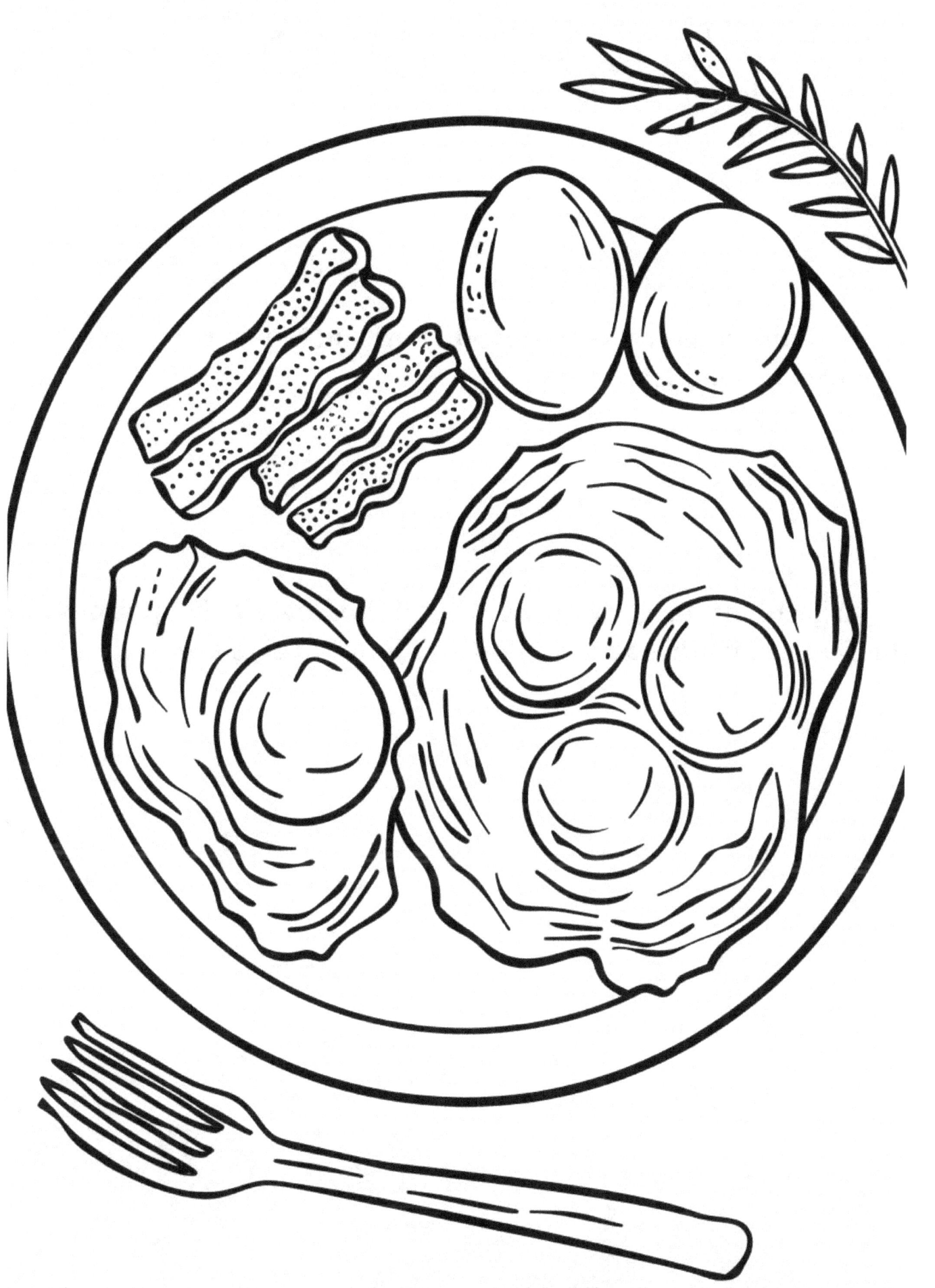

The hamburger as we know it today originated in Hamburg, Germany, in the 19th century.

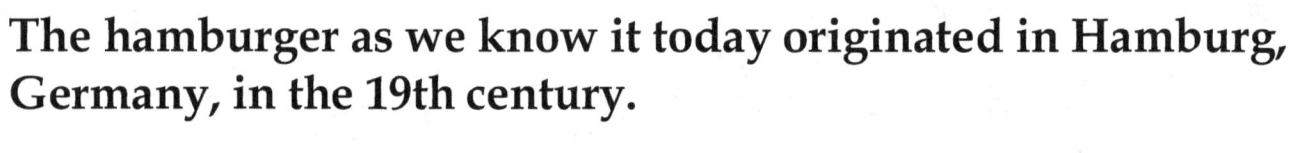

The largest hamburger ever made weighed over 8,000 pounds! Americans consume about 50 billion hamburgers annually.

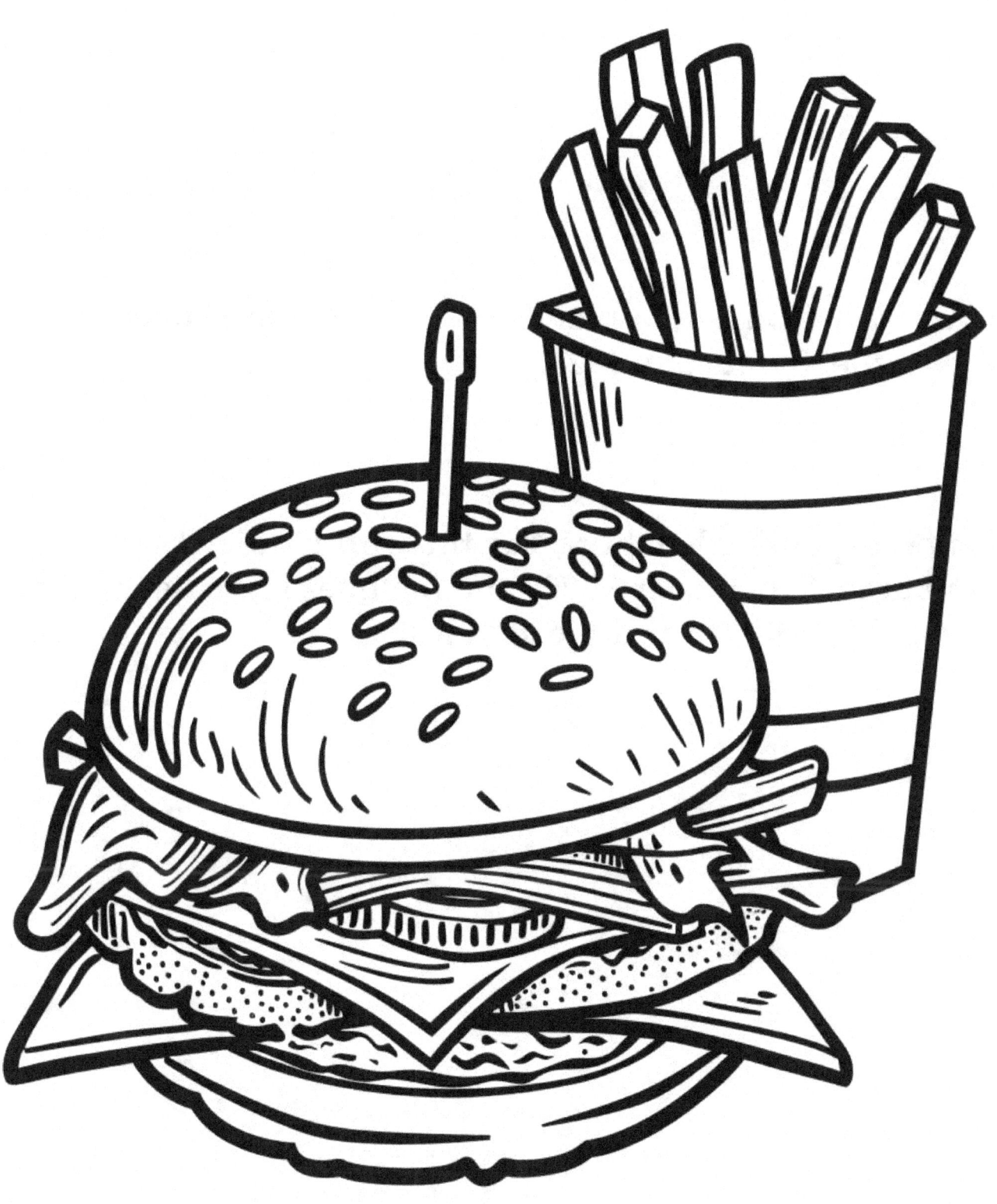

The first fast-food hamburger chain in the United States was White Castle, founded in 1921.

The most expensive hamburger in the world, called the "Glamburger," costs over $1,700 and includes ingredients like Kobe beef, lobster, and edible gold leaf.

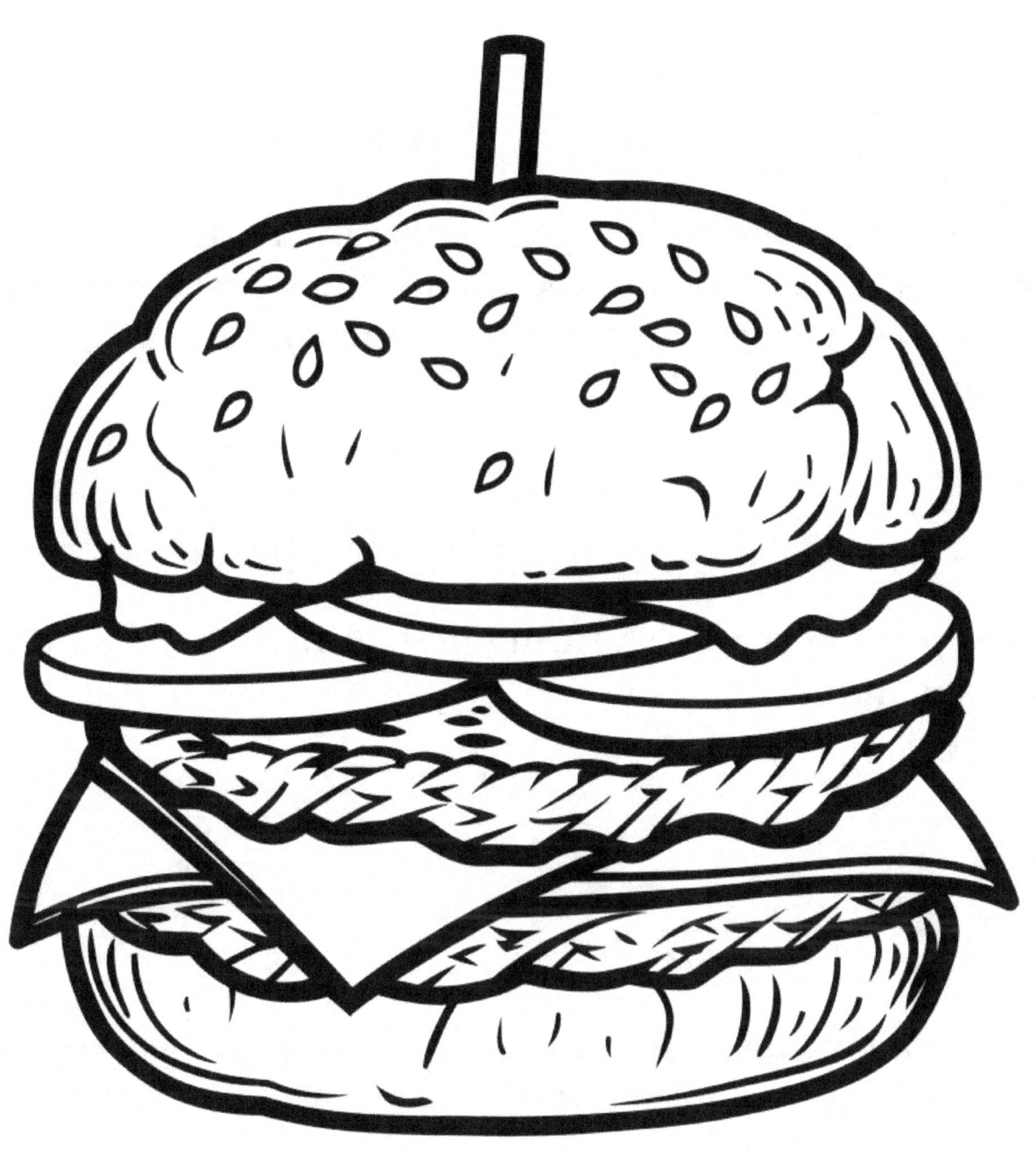

The sandwich is named after John Montagu, the 4th Earl of Sandwich, who reportedly asked for meat to be served between slices of bread so he could eat without interrupting his gambling.

The most popular sandwich filling in the United States is the classic ham and cheese.

The sandwich is considered one of the most versatile foods, with countless variations and combinations enjoyed worldwide.

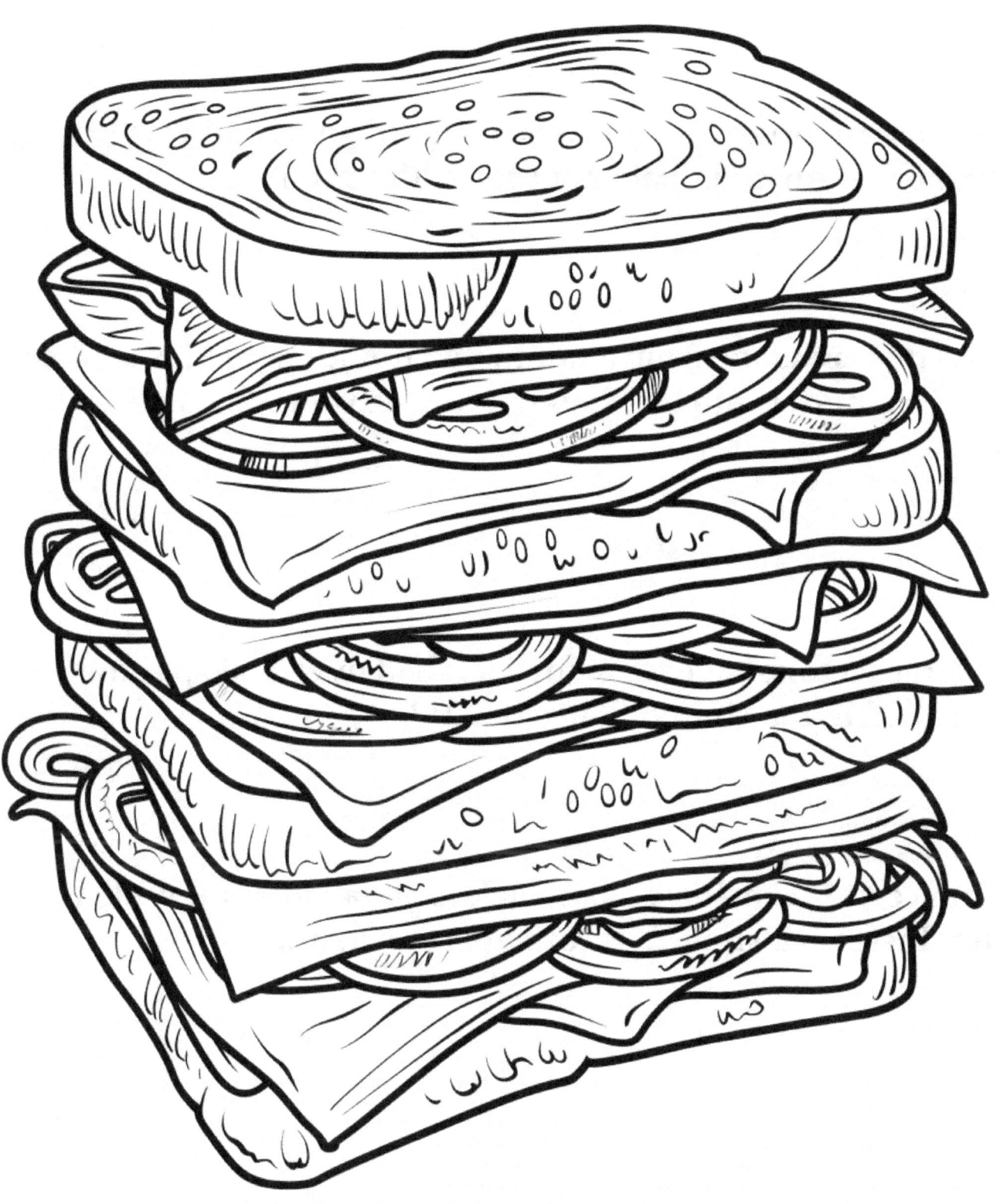

The croissant originated in Austria, not France, and was brought to France by Austrian bakers in the 19th century.

Croissants are made from a laminated dough, which is a process of folding butter into the dough multiple times to create flaky layers.

The largest croissant ever made weighed over 1,000 pounds and was baked in the United States in 2013.

In France, it is considered bad luck to cut a croissant with a knife. Instead, it should be torn apart by hand.

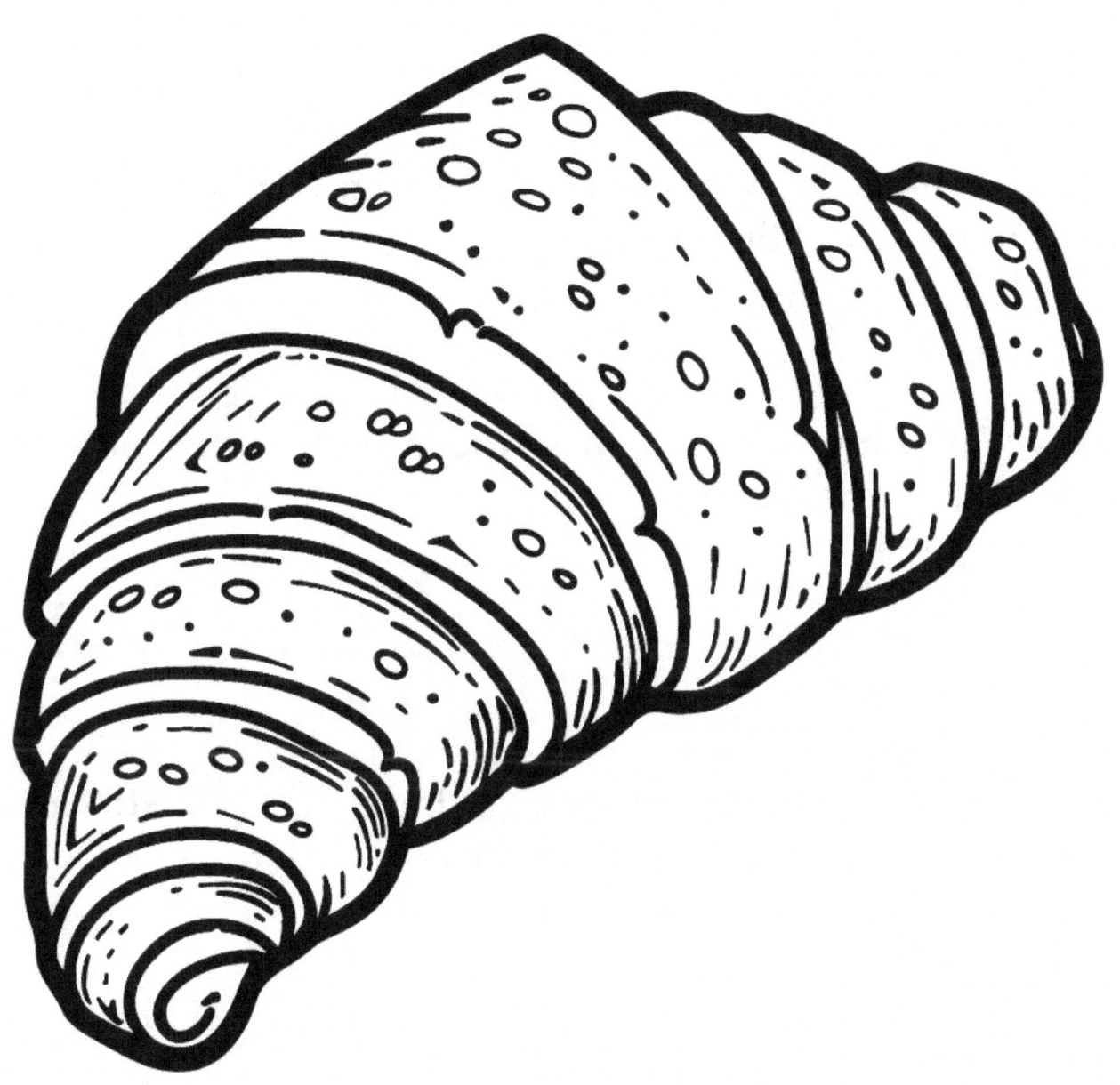

The origin of the hot dog is debated, with claims from both Germany and the United States.

The term "hot dog" is thought to have originated in the United States in the late 19th century.

The world's longest hot dog measured over 600 feet and was made in Japan in 2006.

The most expensive hot dog ever sold was priced at $169 and featured Kobe beef, foie gras, and truffle butter.

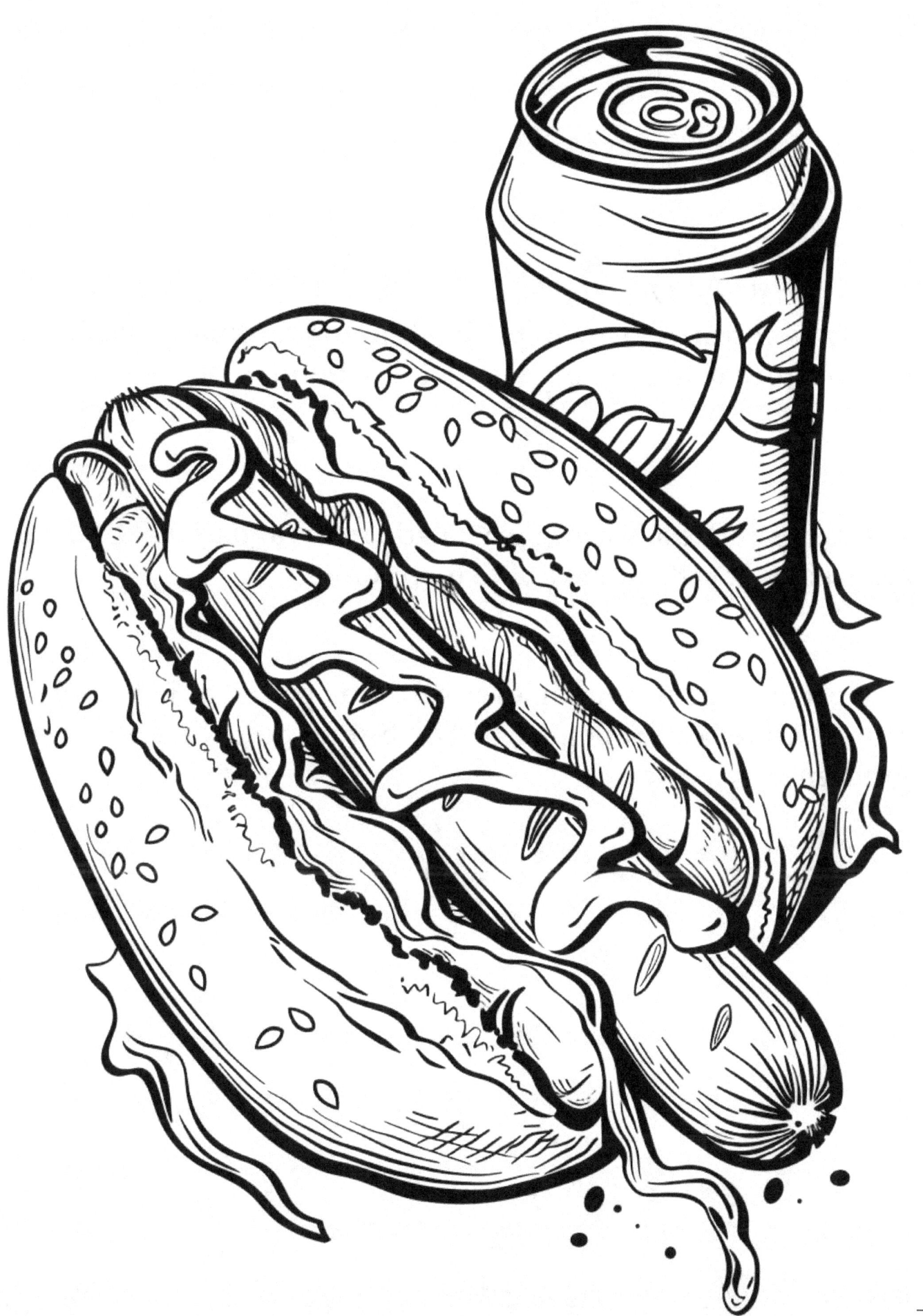

The National Hot Dog and Sausage Council estimates that Americans consume over 20 billion hot dogs annually, with the Fourth of July being the biggest hot dog holiday of the year.

The world's longest hot dog was made in Paraguay in 2011 and measured over 668 meters (2,192 feet) long!

The most expensive hot dog ever sold was priced at $169 and featured Kobe beef, foie gras, truffle butter, and other gourmet ingredients.

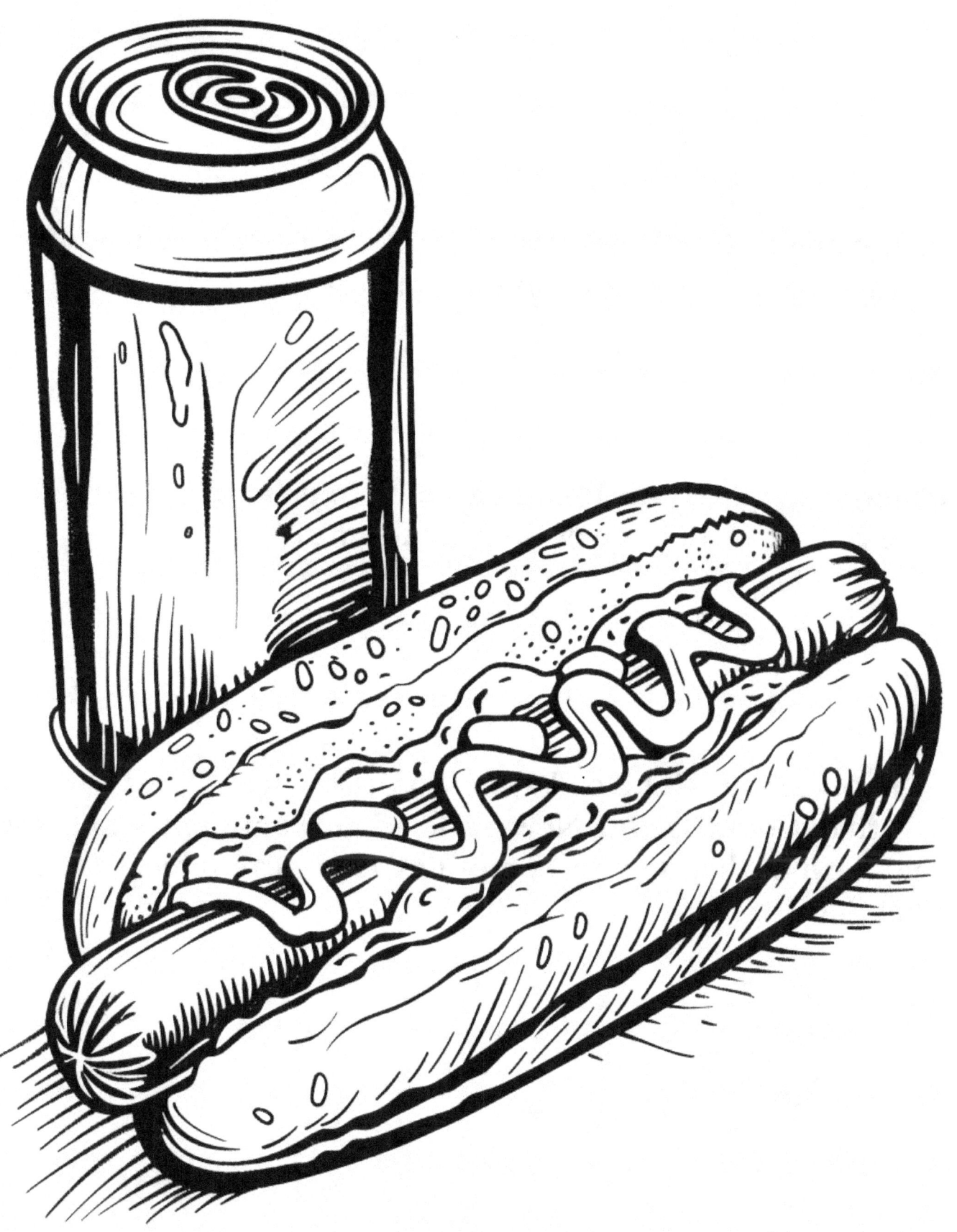

The hot dog is the official state food of Connecticut, where it is often served with mustard, onions, and relish.

The term "hot dog" was first mentioned in print in the United States in 1892 in an issue of the Yale Record.

Nathan's Famous Hot Dog Eating Contest is held annually on July 4th in Coney Island, New York, where contestants compete to eat the most hot dogs in 10 minutes. The current record is over 75 hot dogs!

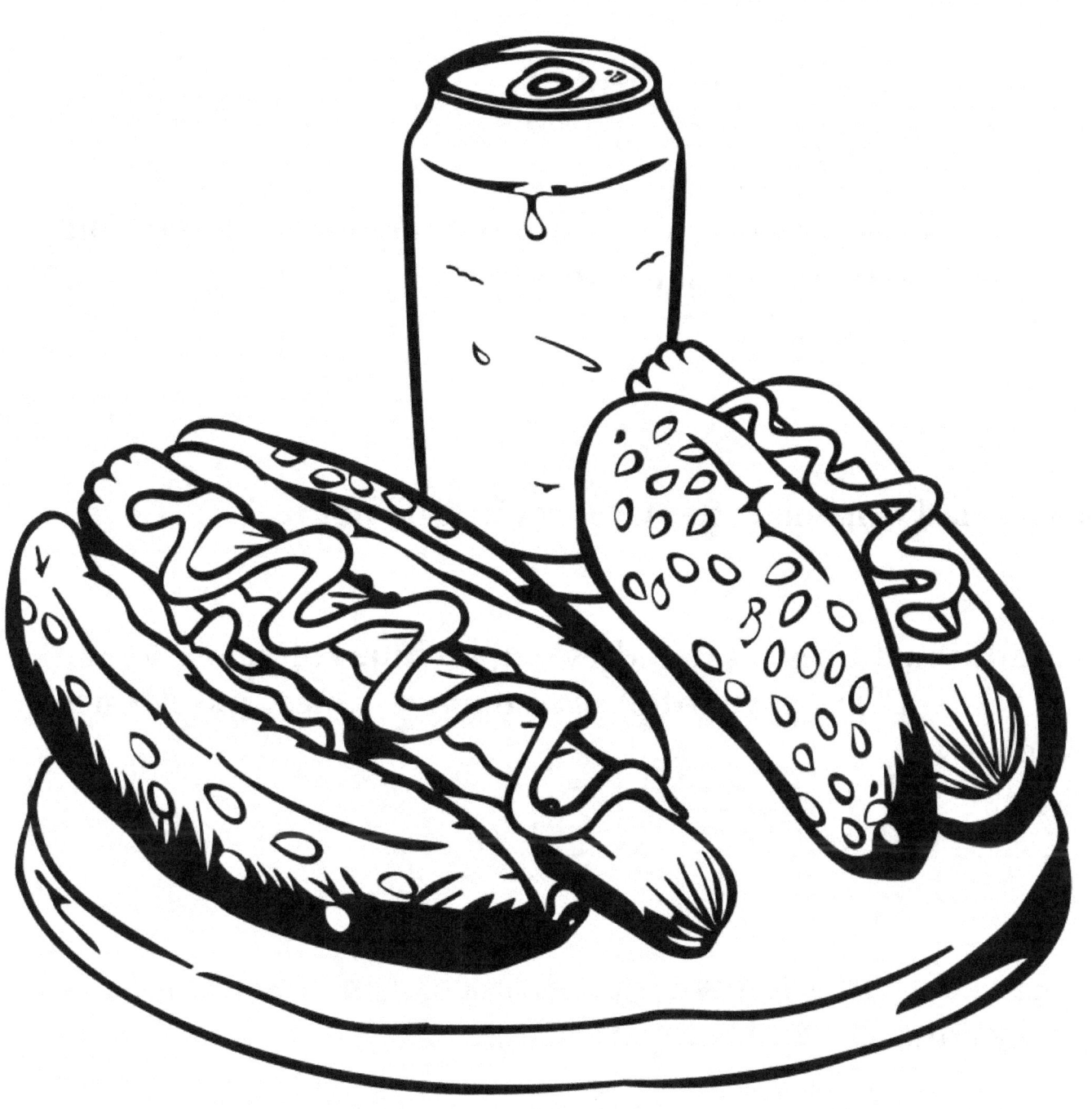

Caesar salad was invented in Tijuana, Mexico, by Italian chef Caesar Cardini in the 1920s.

The original Caesar salad recipe did not include anchovies but relied on Worcestershire sauce for flavor.

Caesar salad is named after Caesar Cardini, not Julius Caesar.

The traditional Caesar salad dressing includes olive oil, lemon juice, garlic, Dijon mustard, Worcestershire sauce, and Parmesan cheese.

The Caesar salad is known for its crunchy romaine lettuce, garlicky croutons, and tangy dressing

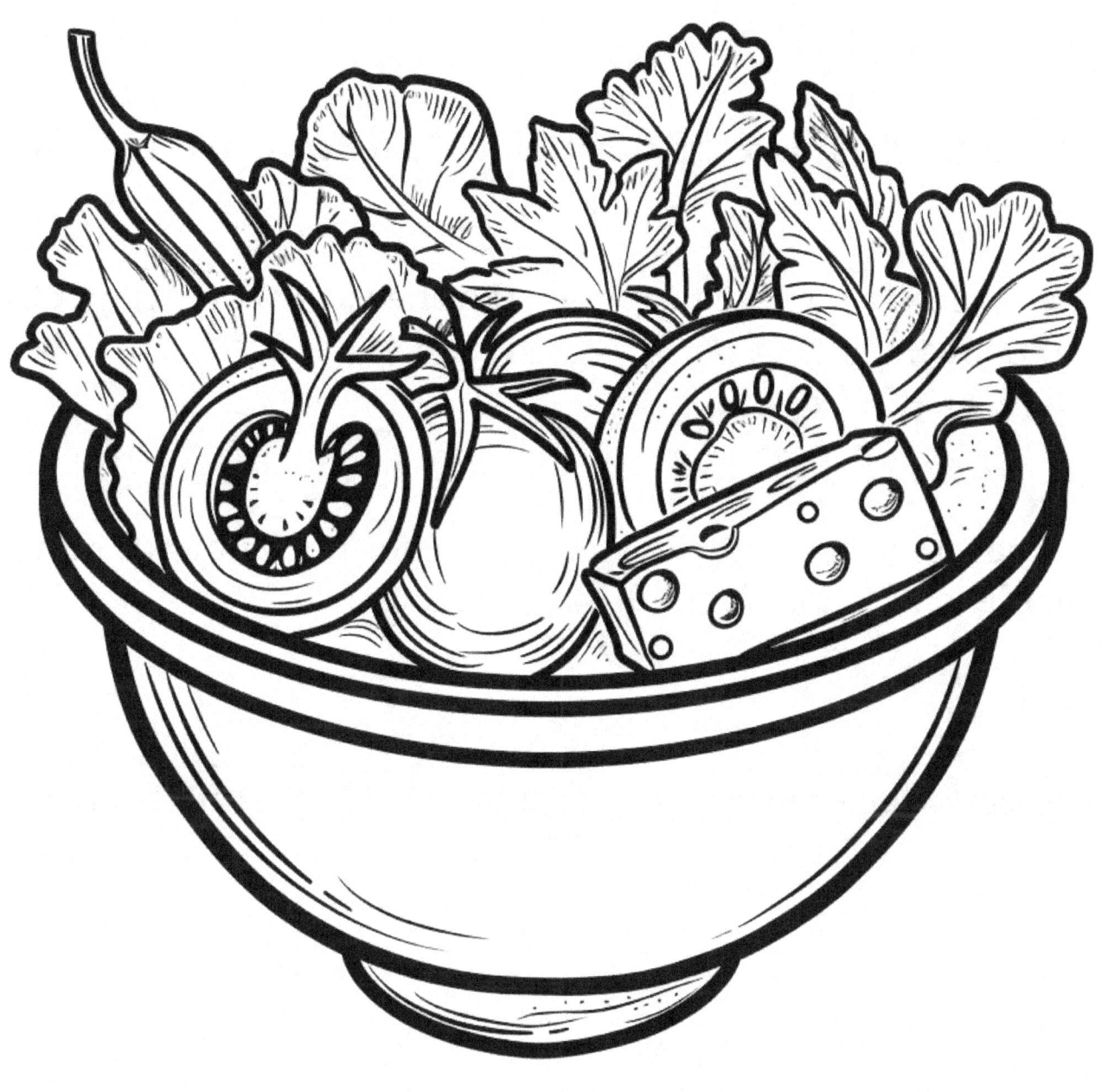

Tachos were first created in 2005 by chef Randy Shaffer at the Minnesota State Fair.

The word "Tachos" is a combination of "tater tots" and "nachos."

Tachos typically include toppings like cheese, bacon, jalapenos, and sour cream.

The largest serving of Tachos weighed over 1,000 pounds and was made in 2017 at a football stadium event.

Tachos are often enjoyed as a popular game day or party snack.

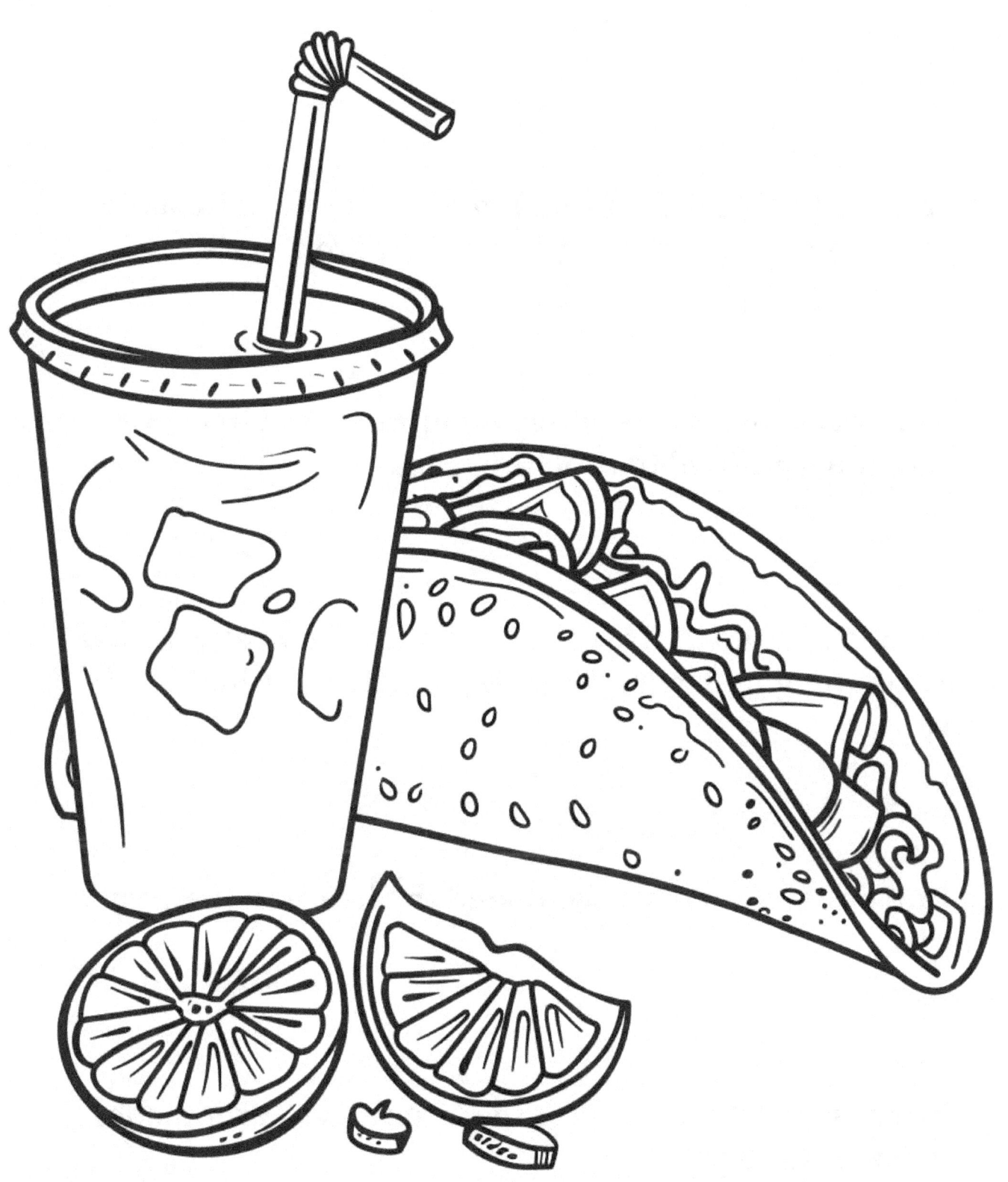

Gyros are a traditional Greek dish made with meat (usually lamb, beef, or chicken) cooked on a vertical rotisserie.

The word "gyro" means "turn" or "revolution" in Greek, referring to the rotating spit used to cook the meat.

Pita bread is a staple in Greek cuisine and is typically served with gyros along with tzatziki sauce, tomatoes, onions, and lettuce.

Gyros are believed to have originated in Greece in the 19th century.

The Guinness World Record for the largest gyro ever made weighed over 1,000 pounds!

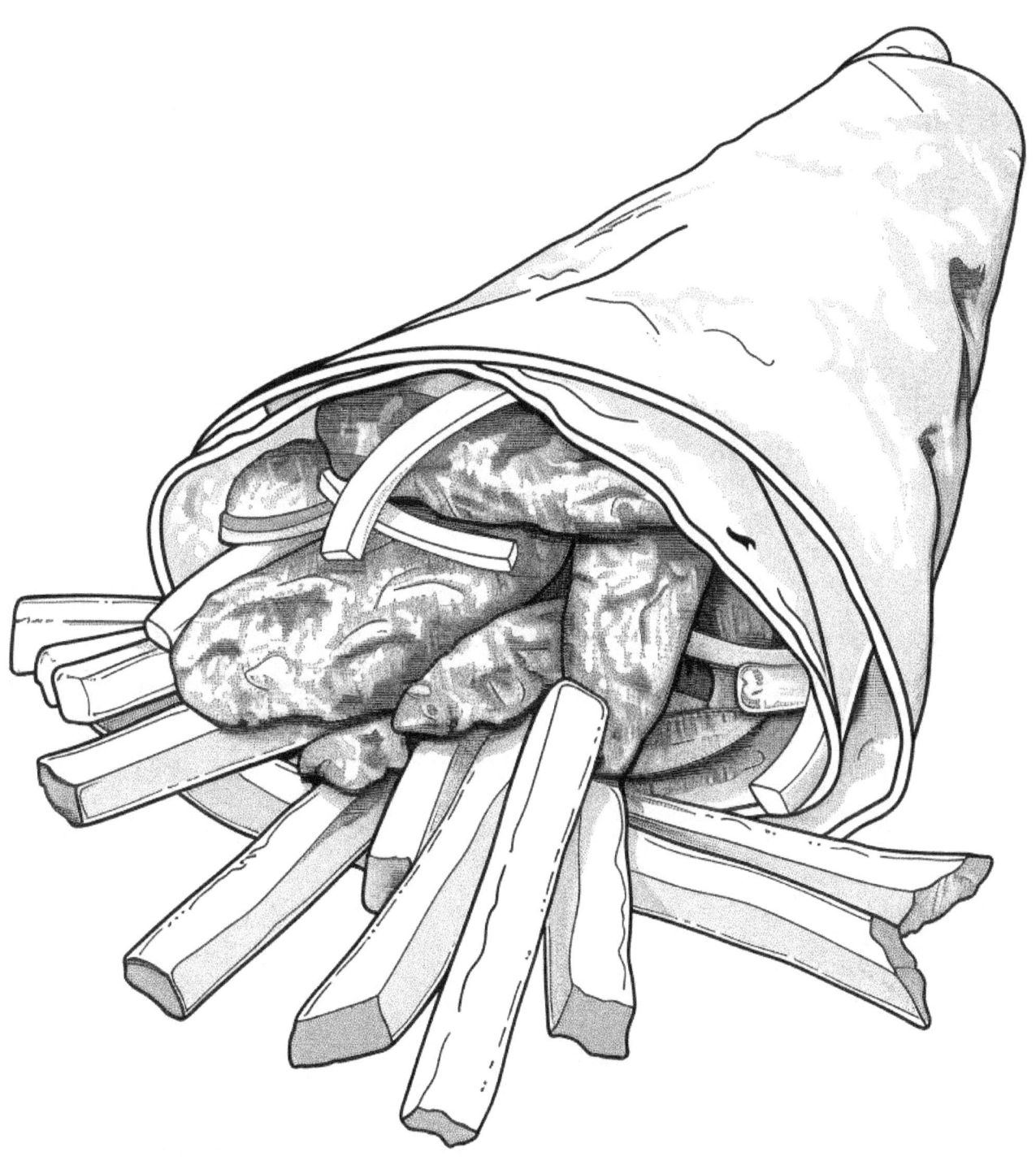

Pizza originated in Naples, Italy, in the 18th century and was initially made with simple ingredients like tomatoes, mozzarella cheese, and basil.

The world's largest pizza ever made measured over 13,000 square feet and was baked in Italy in 2012.

The most expensive pizza ever made, called the "Louis XIII," costs over $12,000 and is topped with caviar, lobster, and truffles

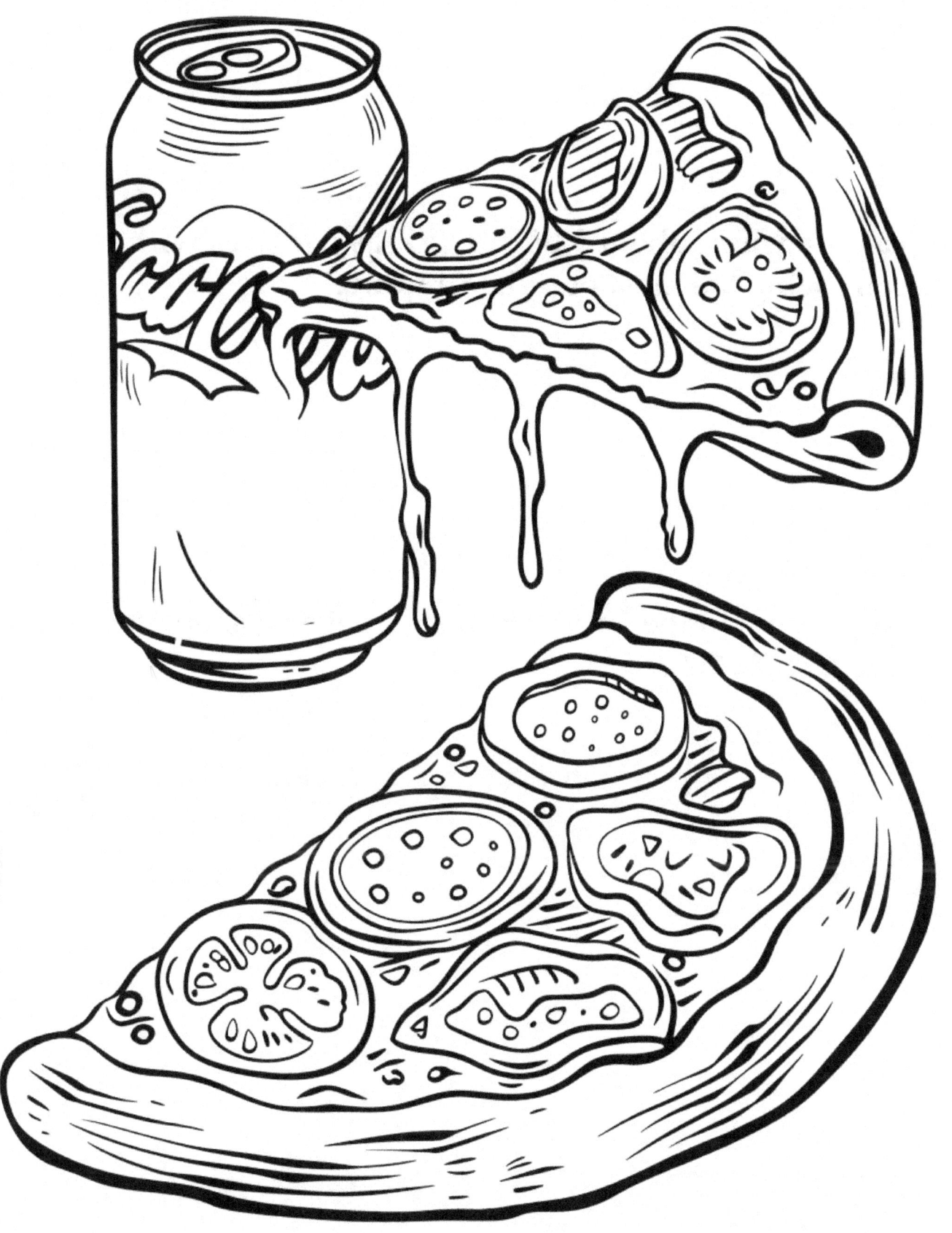

Americans consume about 3 billion pizzas per year, with pepperoni being the most popular topping.

The first pizzeria in the United States, Lombardi's, opened in New York City in 1905.

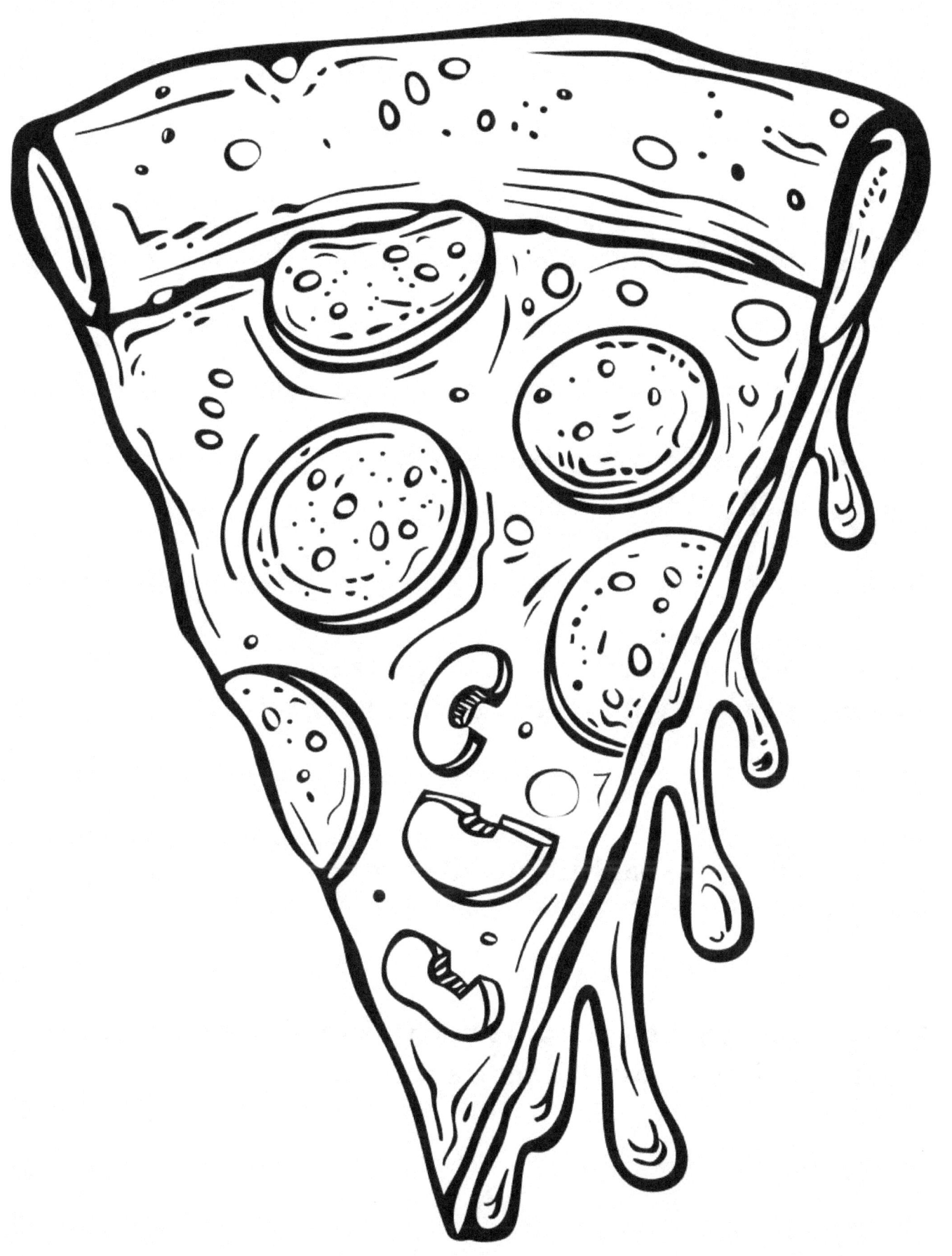

Spaghetti is a type of pasta made from durum wheat semolina and water.

The word "spaghetti" comes from the Italian word "spaghetto," which means "thin string" or "twine."

Spaghetti is one of the most popular pasta shapes worldwide and is commonly served with tomato sauce and meatballs.

The world's longest spaghetti noodle ever made measured over 2 miles long!

In Italy, it is considered impolite to cut spaghetti with a knife, and it is traditionally twirled onto a fork.

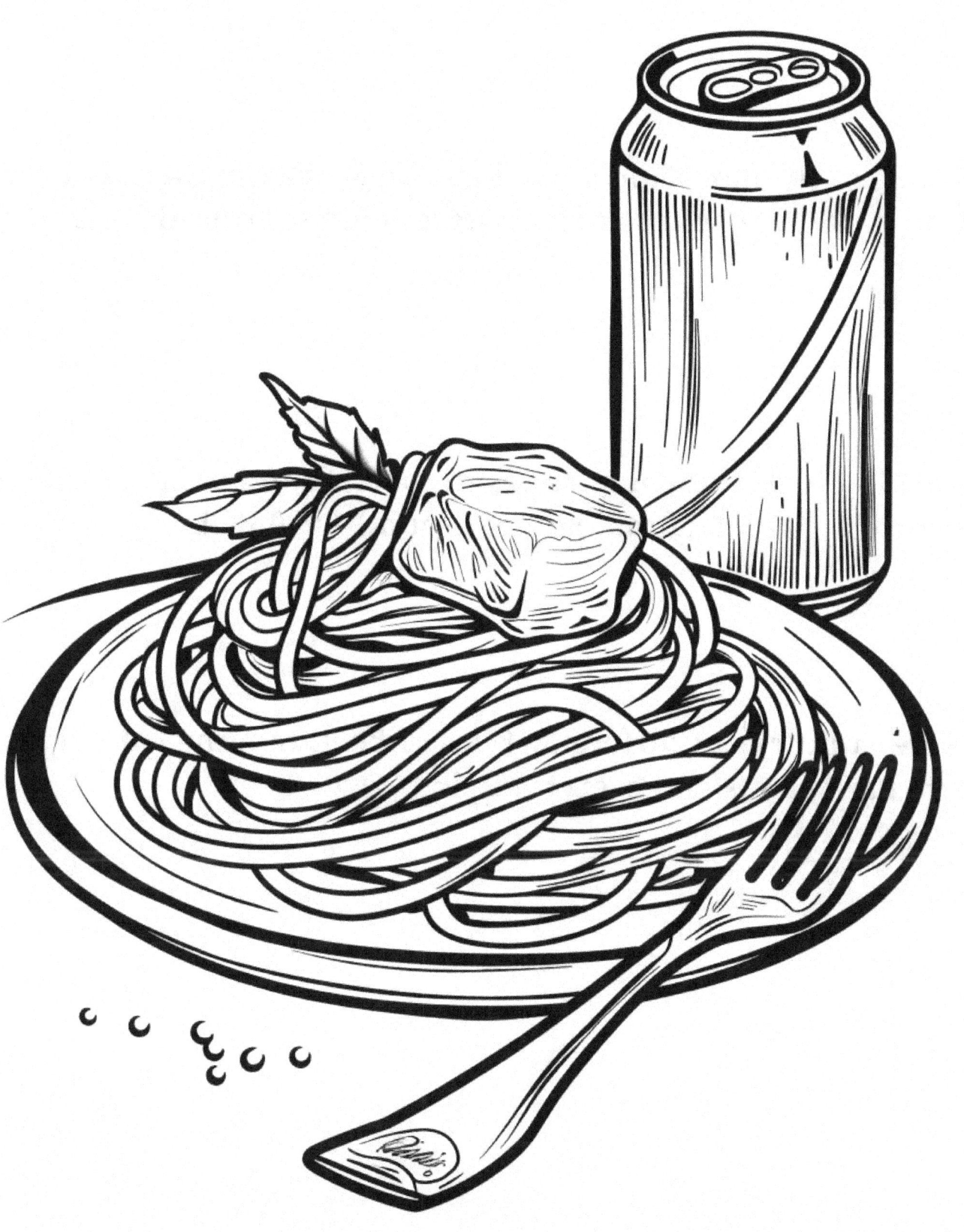

Beer is one of the oldest alcoholic beverages, with evidence of its production dating back to ancient Mesopotamia around 5,000–7,000 BCE.

The world's oldest known recipe is for beer, found on a Sumerian clay tablet dating back to around 4,000 BCE.

There are hundreds of different styles of beer, ranging from light lagers to dark stouts and everything in between.

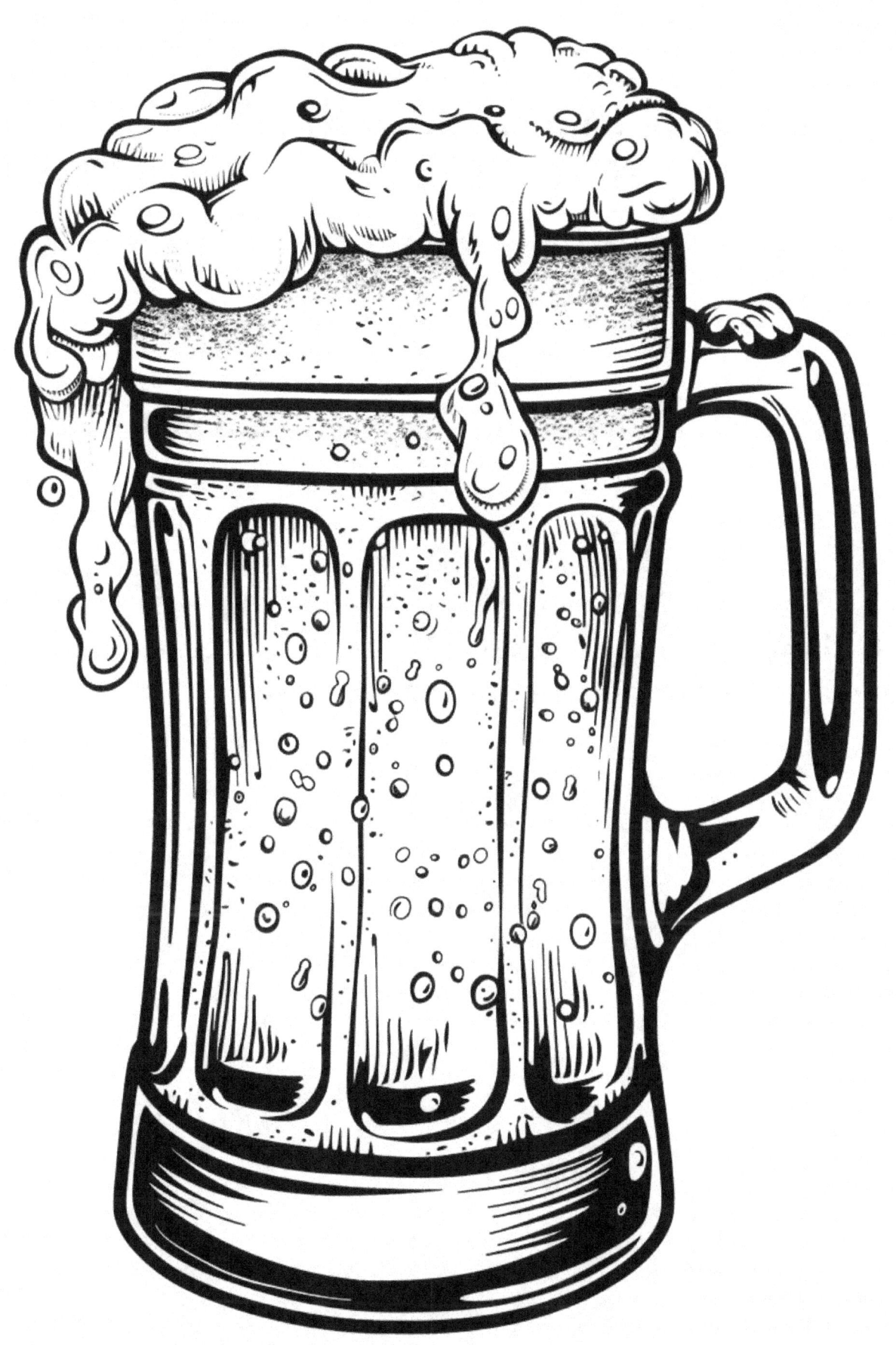

The Czech Republic consumes the most beer per capita in the world, with an average of over 140 liters per person per year.

The study of beer and beer-making is called zythology.

The Guinness World Record for the largest beer tasting event involved 1,236 participants and was achieved in Spain in 2016.

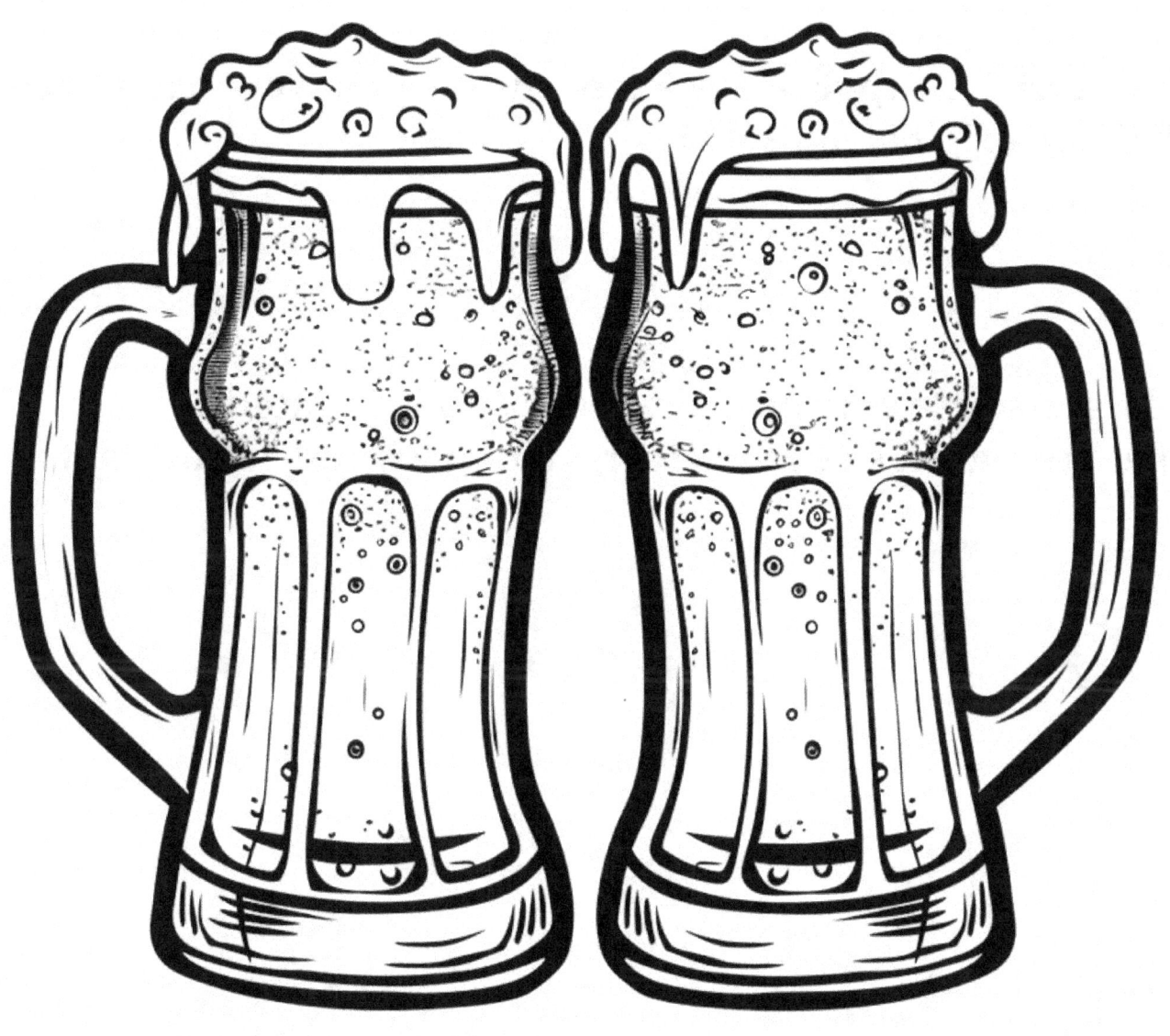

Apples are one of the most widely cultivated fruits in the world. There are over 7,500 known varieties of apples, ranging in color, size, and flavor.

The proverb "An apple a day keeps the doctor away" dates back to 1866 and originated in Wales.

The largest apple ever picked weighed over 4 pounds!
Apples are a good source of fiber, vitamin C, and antioxidants

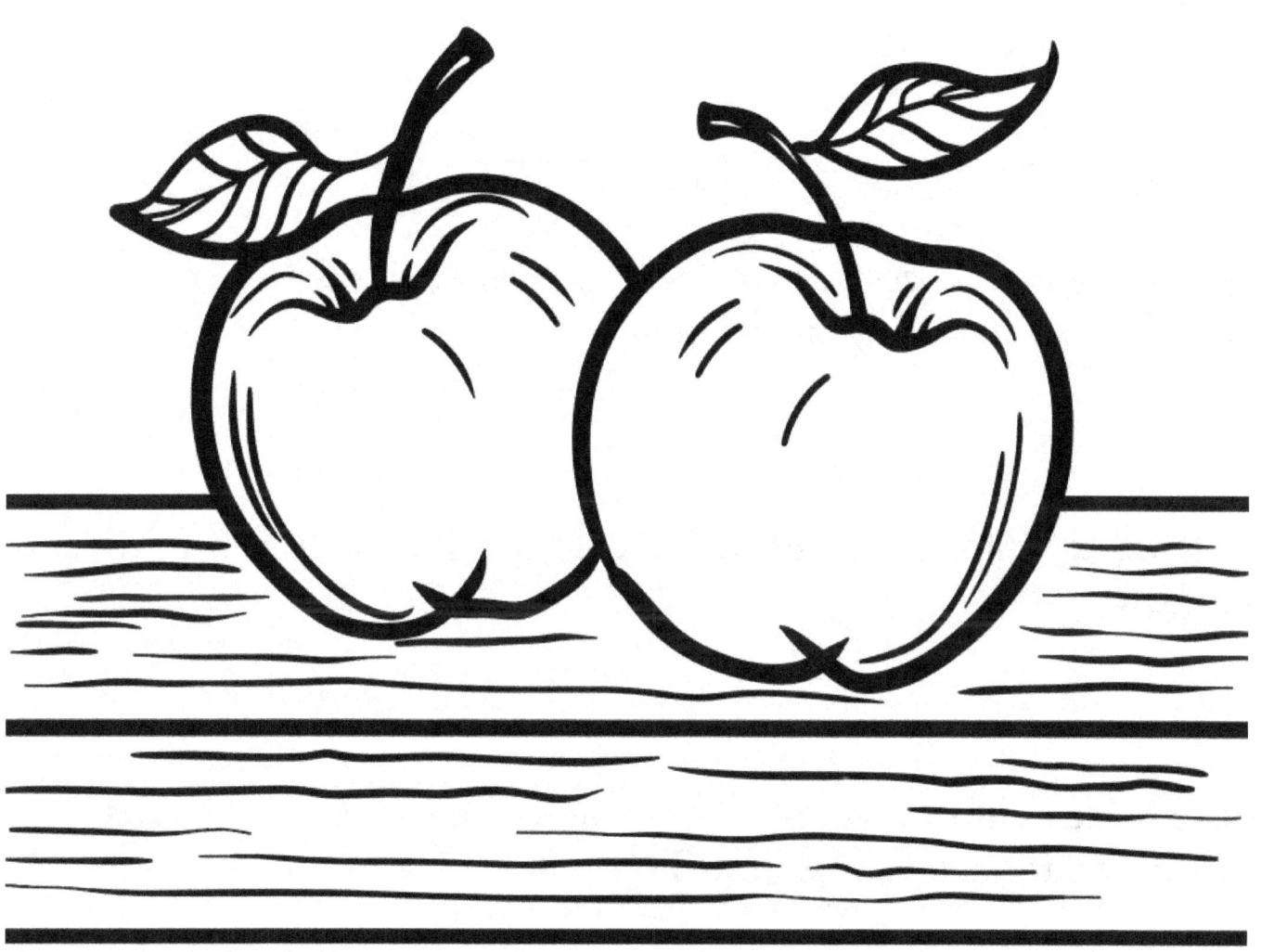

Apple juice is made by pressing and extracting the juice from apples.

The first apple juice press was invented in the United States in the 19th century.

Apple juice can be consumed fresh or pasteurized and is often enjoyed as a refreshing beverage.

The United States is one of the largest producers of apple juice in the world.

Apple juice can be used as a base for cocktails and mocktails, adding natural sweetness and flavor

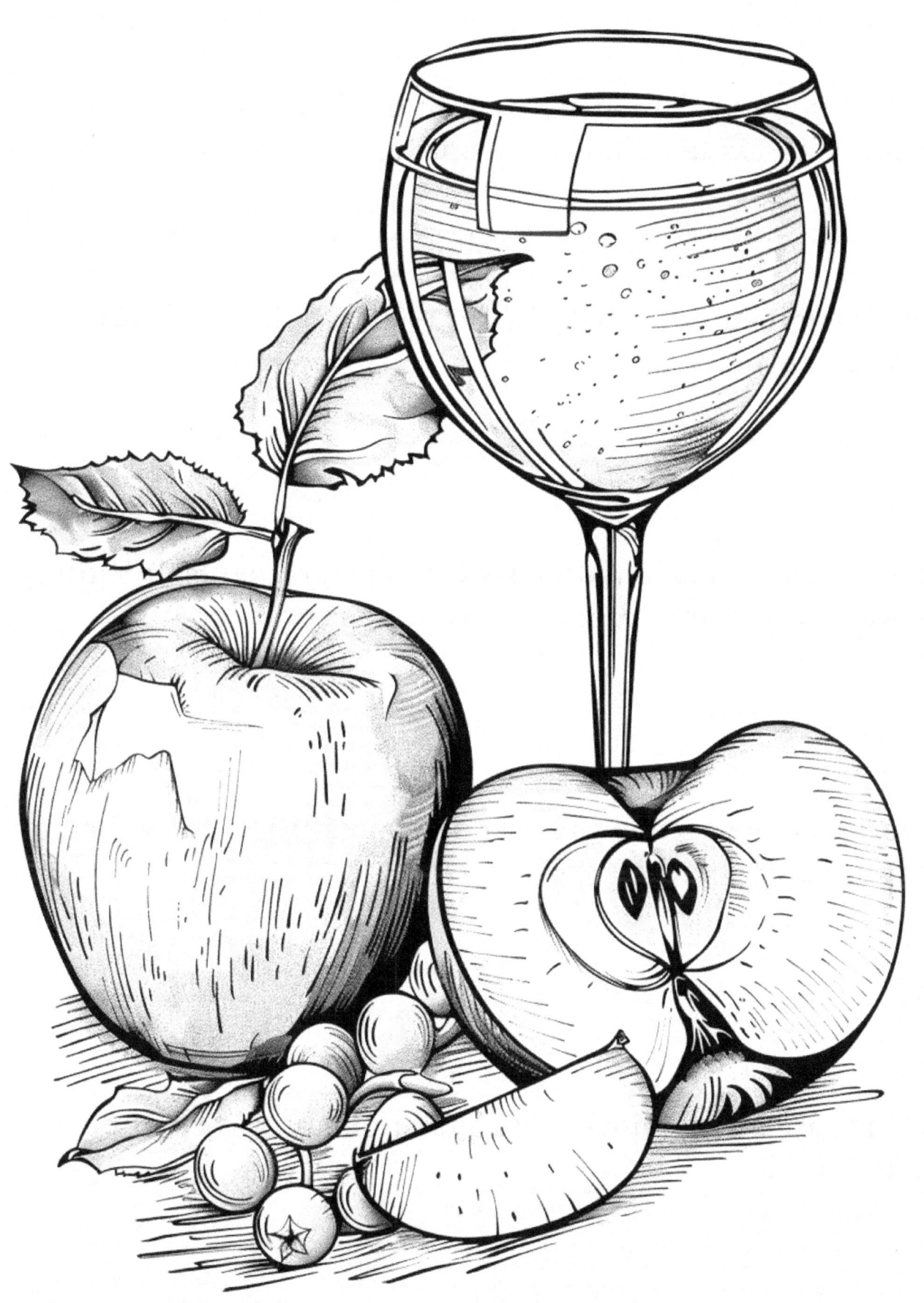

The term "smoothie" was first used in the 1960s to describe a blended drink made with fruit, yogurt, and other ingredients.

Smoothies gained popularity in the 1990s as a healthy and convenient beverage option.

Smoothies can be made with a variety of ingredients, including fruits, vegetables, yogurt, milk, and protein powder.

The world's largest smoothie was made in 2010 and weighed over 13,000 pounds!

Smoothies are often enjoyed as a nutritious breakfast or post-workout snack.

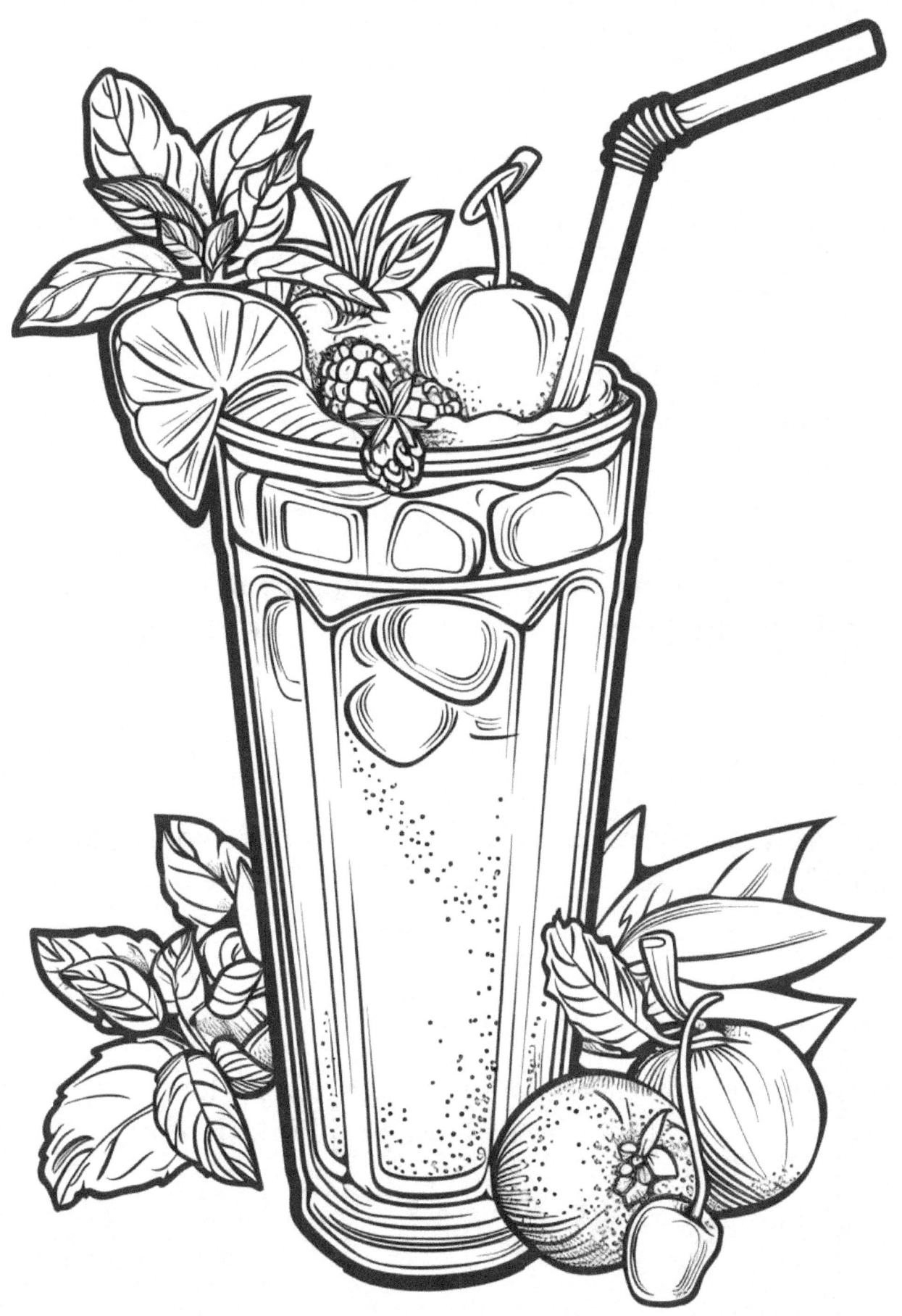

Salmon is a popular fish species prized for its flavorful and nutritious flesh.

Salmon are born in freshwater rivers, migrate to the ocean to mature, and then return to their birthplace to spawn.

Wild-caught salmon is known for its vibrant color and rich flavor, while farmed salmon is more readily available and affordable.

Salmon is a great source of omega-3 fatty acids, protein, and vitamin D.

There are several species of salmon, including Atlantic, Chinook (King), Sockeye (Red), Coho (Silver), and Pink (Humpy).

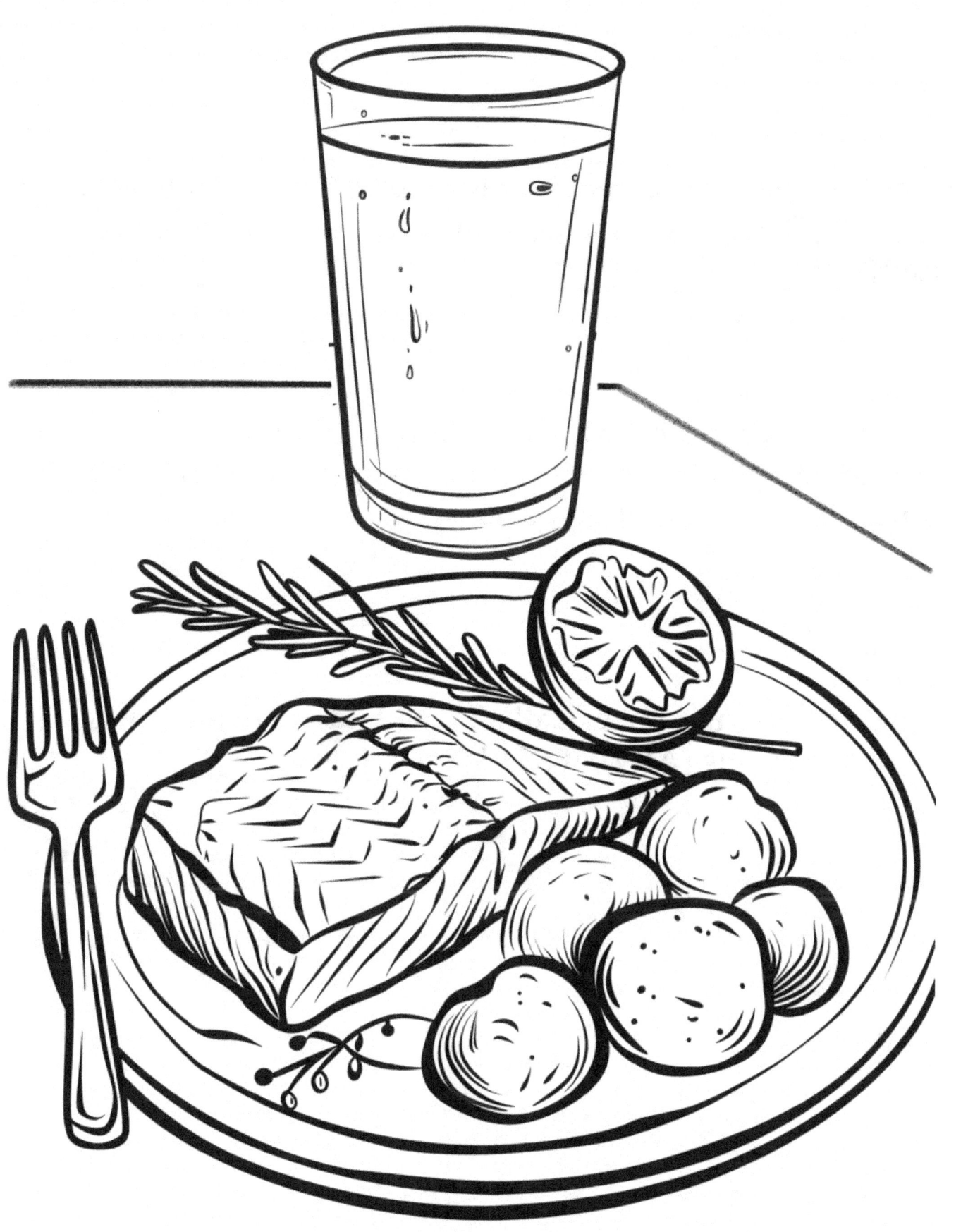

The oldest operating brewery in the world is the Weihenstephan Brewery in Bavaria, Germany, which has been brewing beer since 1040.

The ancient Sumerians, who lived in what is now Iraq, worshipped a goddess of beer named Ninkasi and included hymns to her in their religious texts

The world's strongest beer, called "The End of History," has an alcohol by volume (ABV) of 55%!

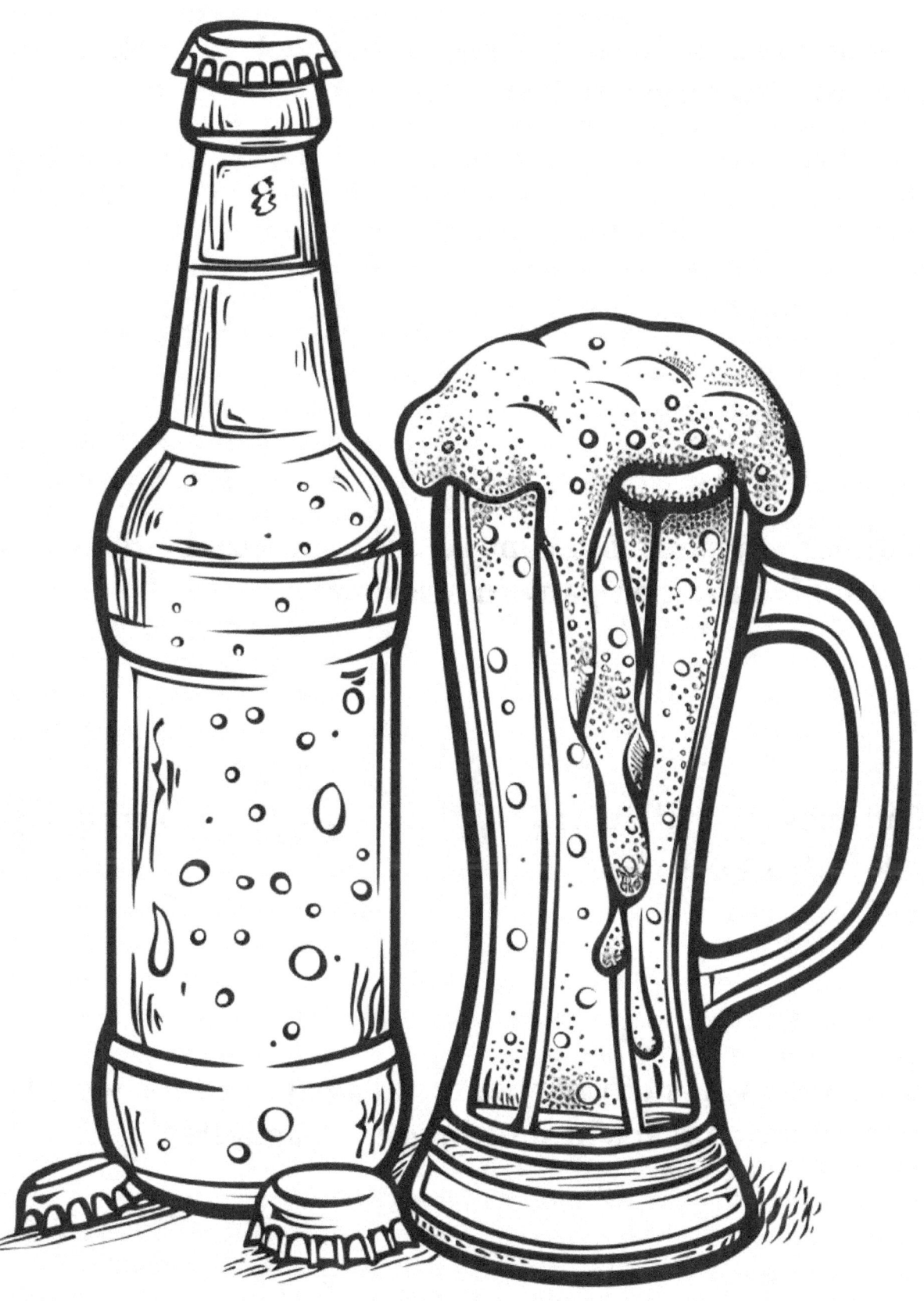

Bread is one of the oldest prepared foods, dating back to ancient civilizations like Egypt and Mesopotamia.

The earliest evidence of bread-making dates back over 14,000 years.

Sliced bread was first sold commercially in 1928 by the Chillicothe Baking Company in Missouri.

The Guinness World Record for the largest bread sculpture is over 5,000 pounds!

There are thousands of varieties of bread around the world, ranging from flatbreads to sourdough to baguettes

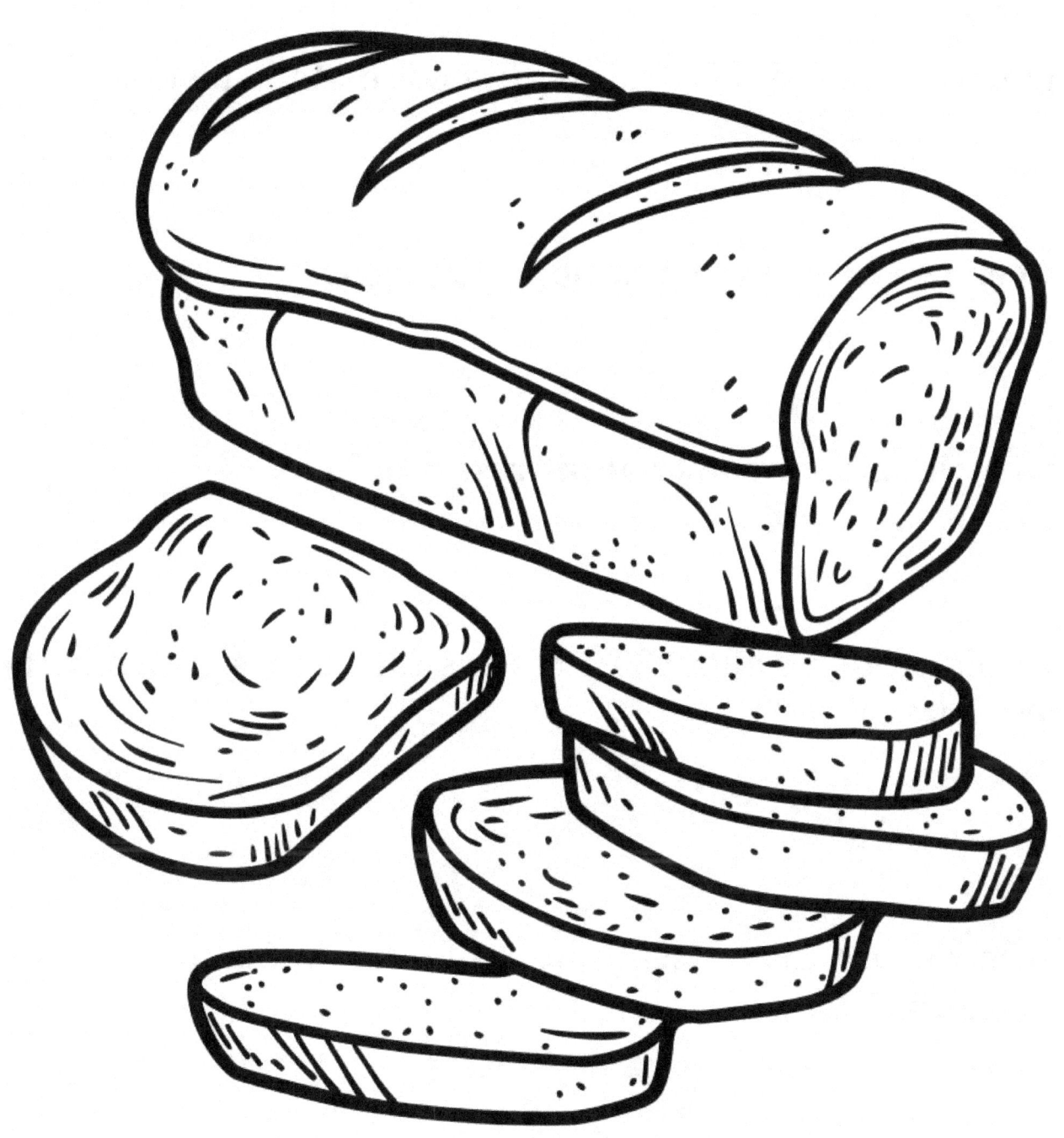

Strawberries are the only fruit with seeds on the outside.

The average strawberry has around 200 seeds.

Strawberries are a member of the rose family.

California produces about 80% of the strawberries grown in the United States.

Strawberries are an excellent source of vitamin C and antioxidants.

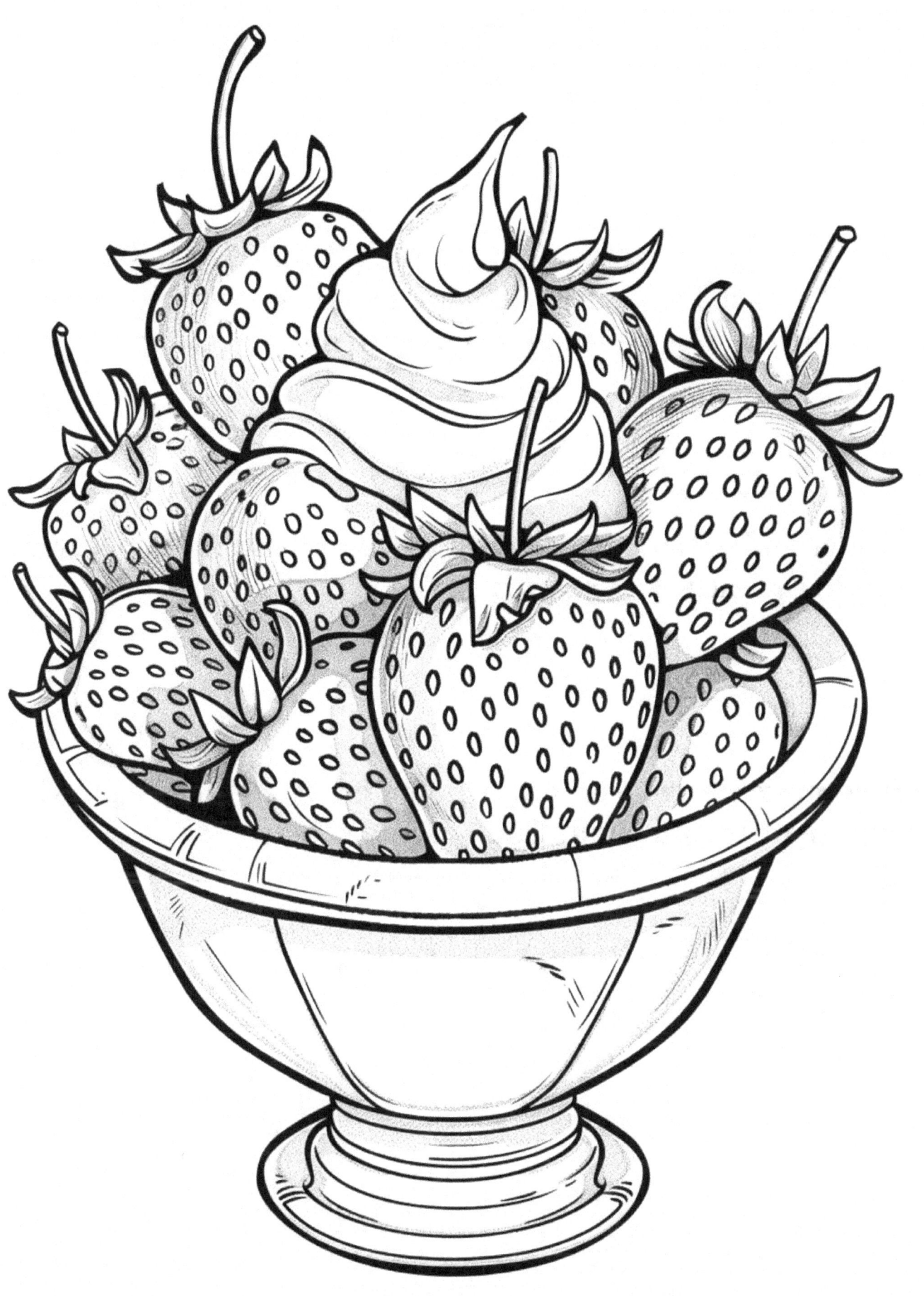

The term "milkshake" was first used in the late 19th century to describe an alcoholic beverage made with milk, eggs, and whiskey.

The modern milkshake, made with ice cream and milk, became popular in the early 20th century.

The first milkshake machine was invented by a Walgreens employee named Ivar "Pop" Coulson in 1922

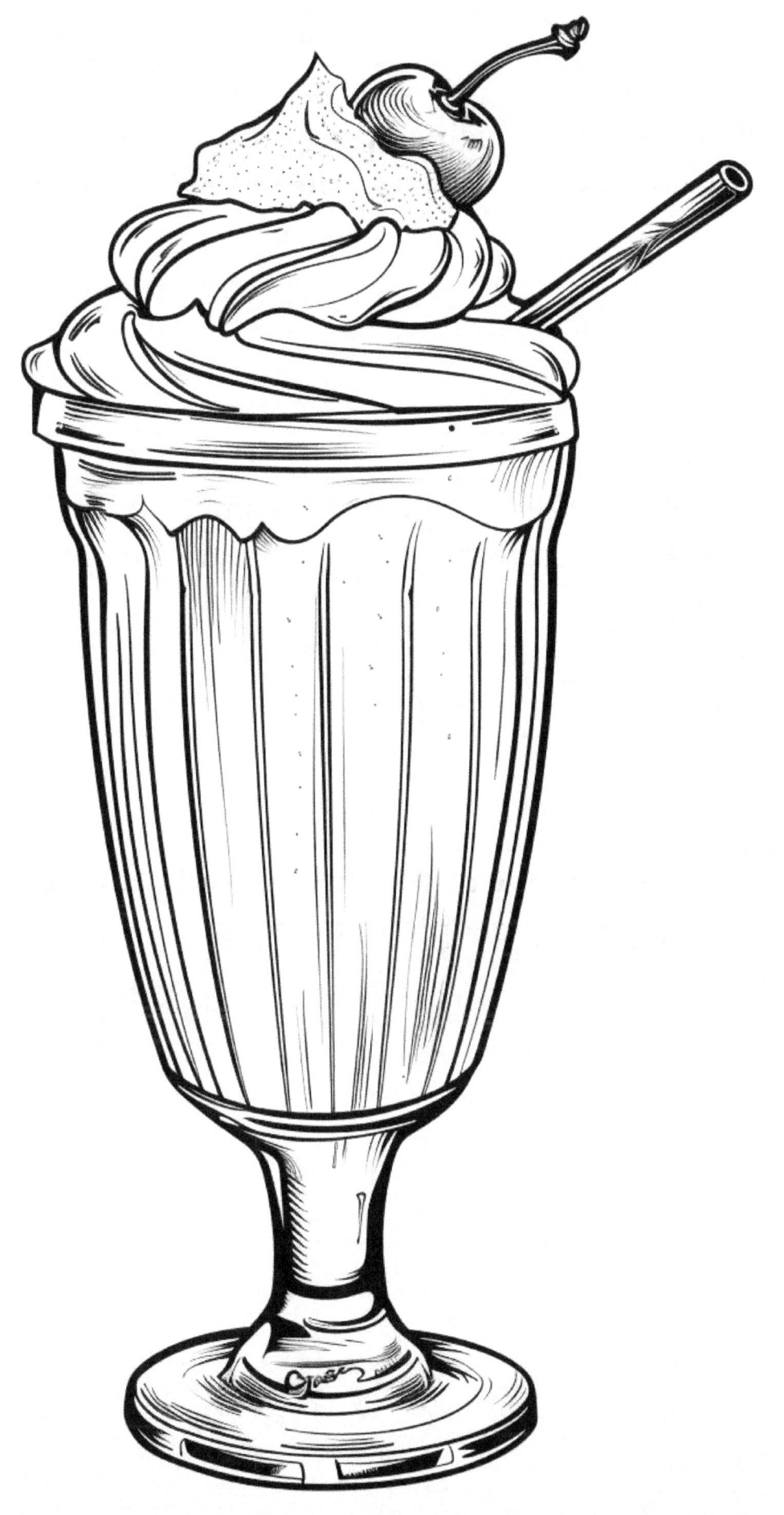

The first chocolate cake recipe appeared in 1764 in a book titled "The Art of Cookery Made Plain and Easy" by Hannah Glasse.

German chocolate cake is not from Germany but is named after Samuel German, who created a type of dark baking chocolate in 1852.

The chocolate cake is one of the most popular desserts worldwide, enjoyed by people of all ages.

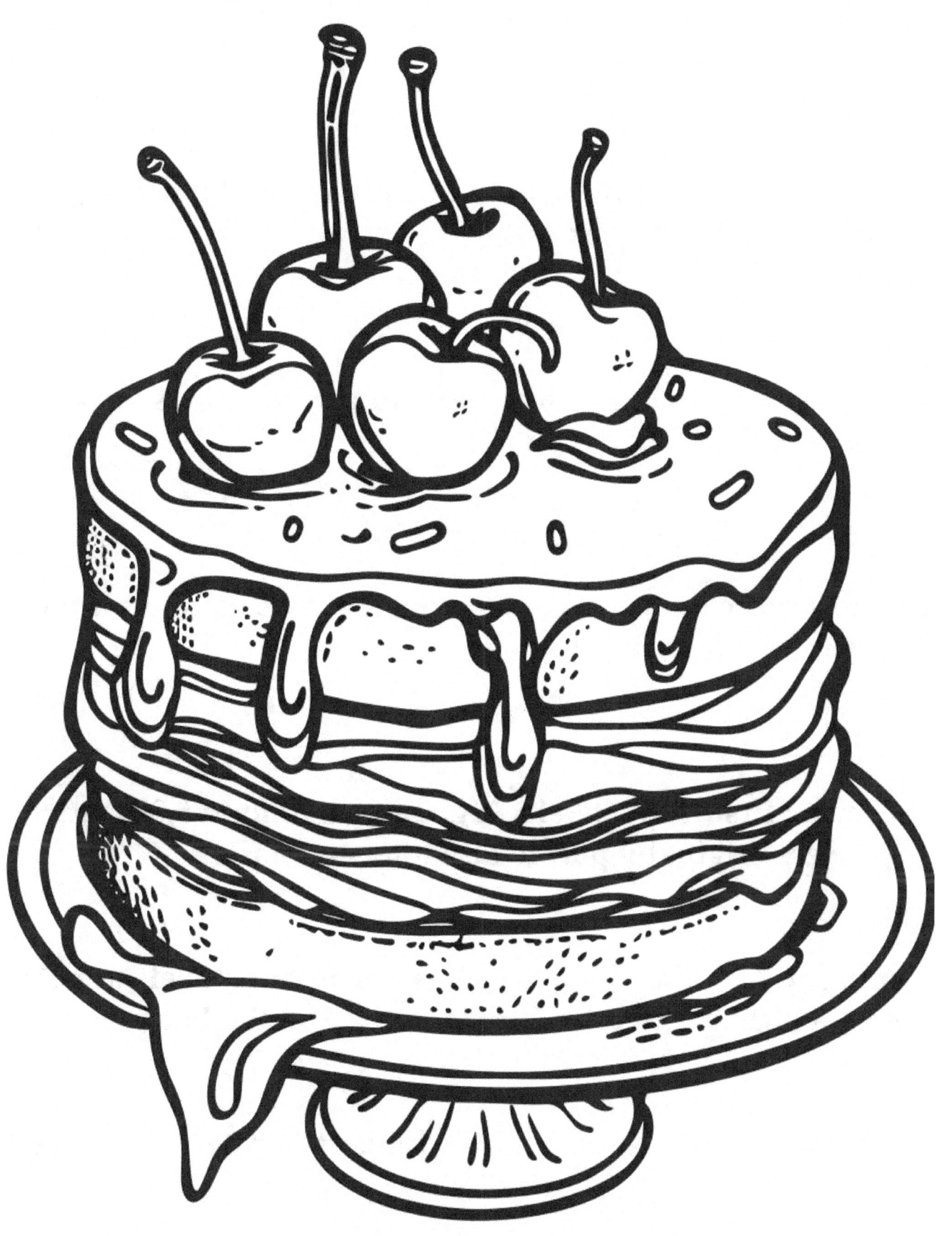

The name "broccoli" comes from the Italian word "broccolo," which means "cabbage sprout."

Broccoli is rich in vitamins, minerals, and antioxidants, making it a nutritious addition to any diet.

The largest broccoli ever recorded weighed over 35 pounds and was grown in Alaska in 1993.

Carrots:

Carrots were first cultivated in Afghanistan around 5,000 years ago and were originally purple or white, not orange.

The orange color of modern carrots is due to high levels of beta-carotene, which is converted into vitamin A in the body.

The Guinness World Record for the longest carrot ever recorded is over 19 feet!

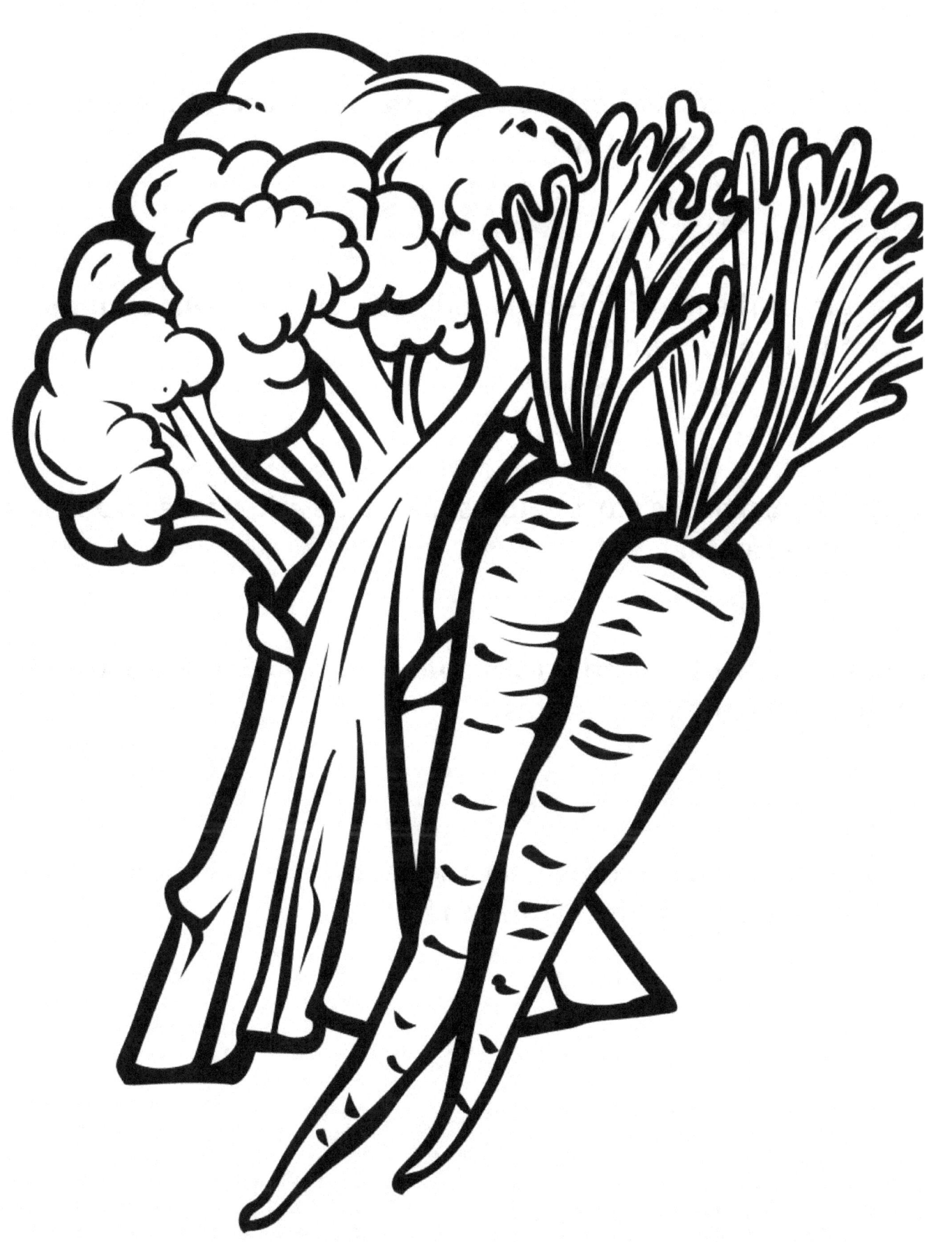

The martini is a cocktail made with gin and vermouth, garnished with an olive or a lemon twist.

The origin of the martini is debated, with claims from both the United States and Europe.

The classic martini is stirred, not shaken, despite James Bond's famous preference.

The most expensive martini ever sold was priced at $10,000 and included a diamond as a garnish.

The martini is known for its elegance and sophistication and has been featured in countless films and books

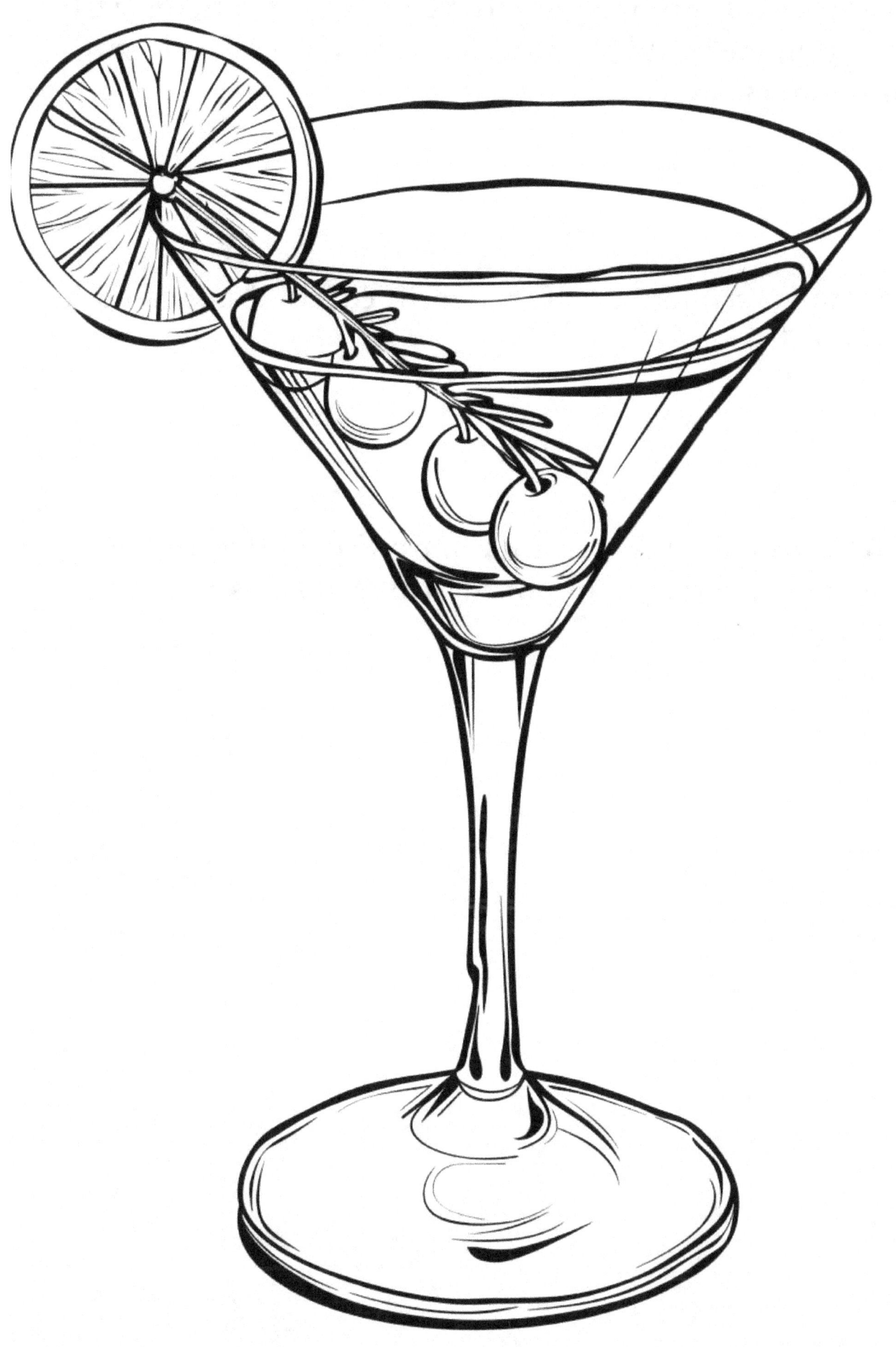

The word "cocktail" originated in the United States in the early 19th century and referred to a mixed drink with spirits, sugar, water, and bitters.

The first known printed use of the word "cocktail" appeared in a newspaper in 1806.

Cocktails became popular during Prohibition in the United States when people turned to mixed drinks to mask the taste of bootlegged alcohol.

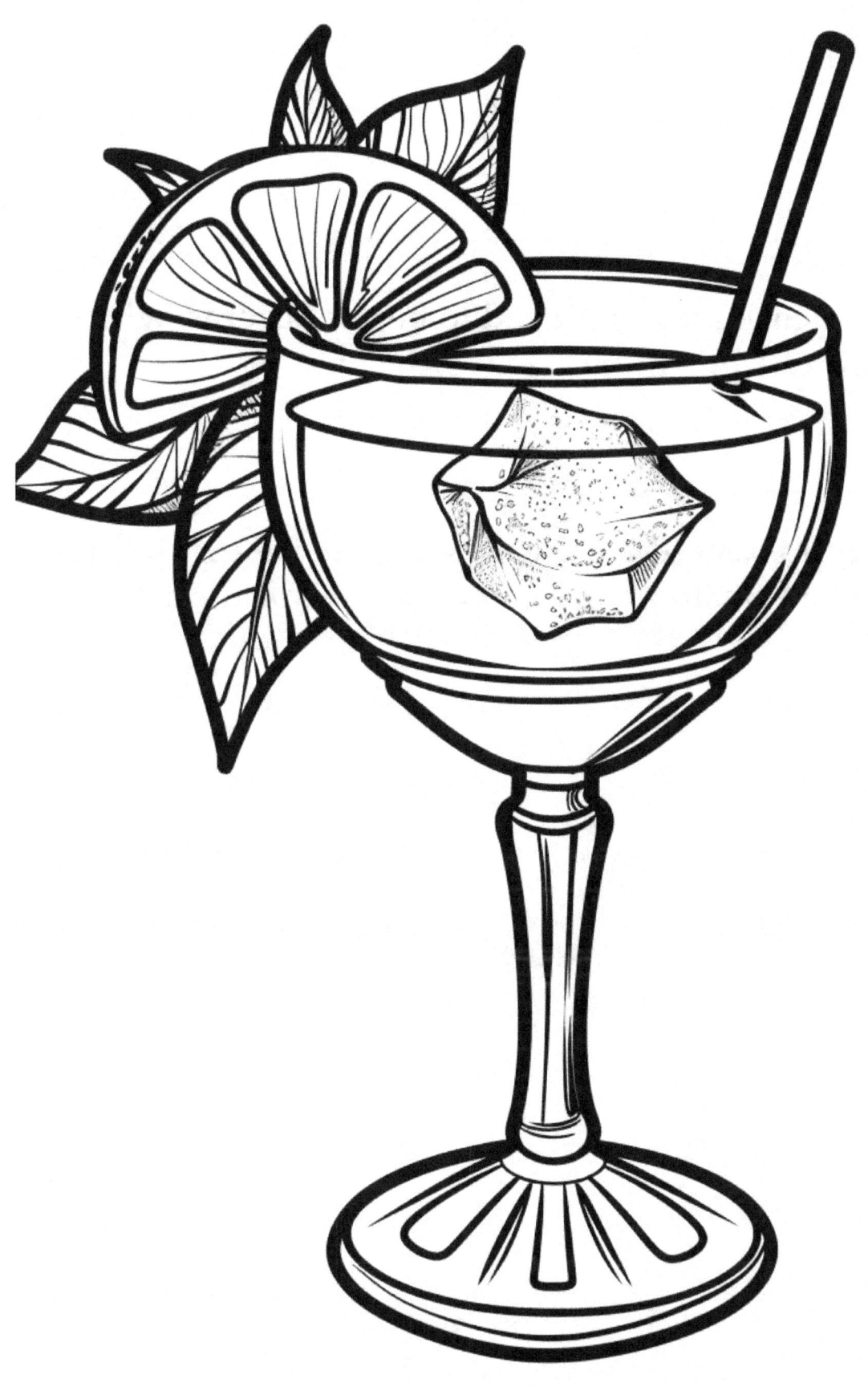

The world's oldest cocktail is believed to be the Sazerac, which originated in New Orleans in the early 19th century.

The Guinness World Record for the most expensive cocktail is $12,970, called "The Winston," and contains rare spirits and ingredients.

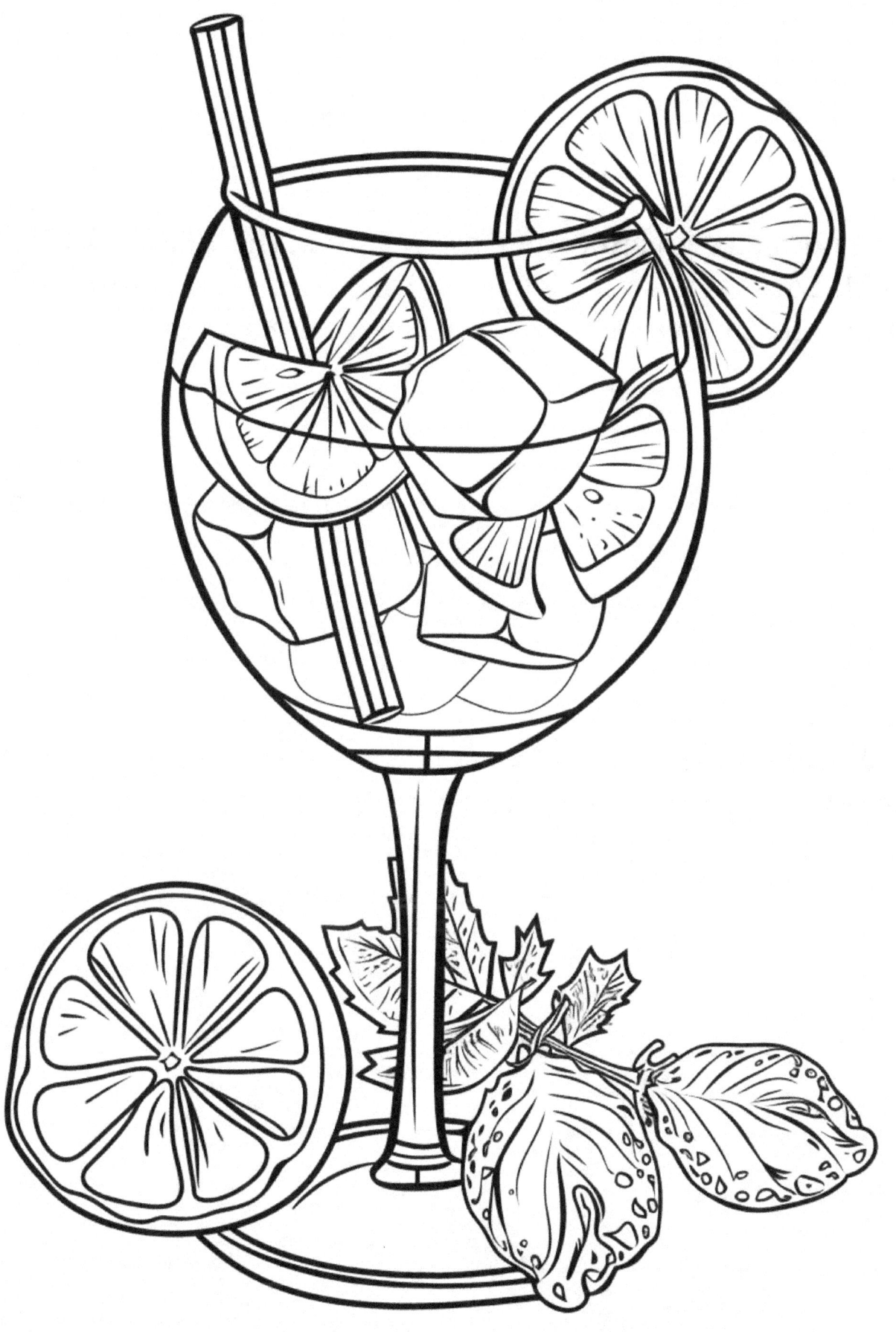

he first known ice cream cone was created at the 1904 World's Fair in St. Louis, Missouri, when an ice cream vendor ran out of cups and rolled up waffles to serve the ice cream instead.

It takes an average of 50 licks to finish a single scoop ice cream cone.

July is National Ice Cream Month in the United States, with National Ice Cream Day celebrated on the third Sunday of July.

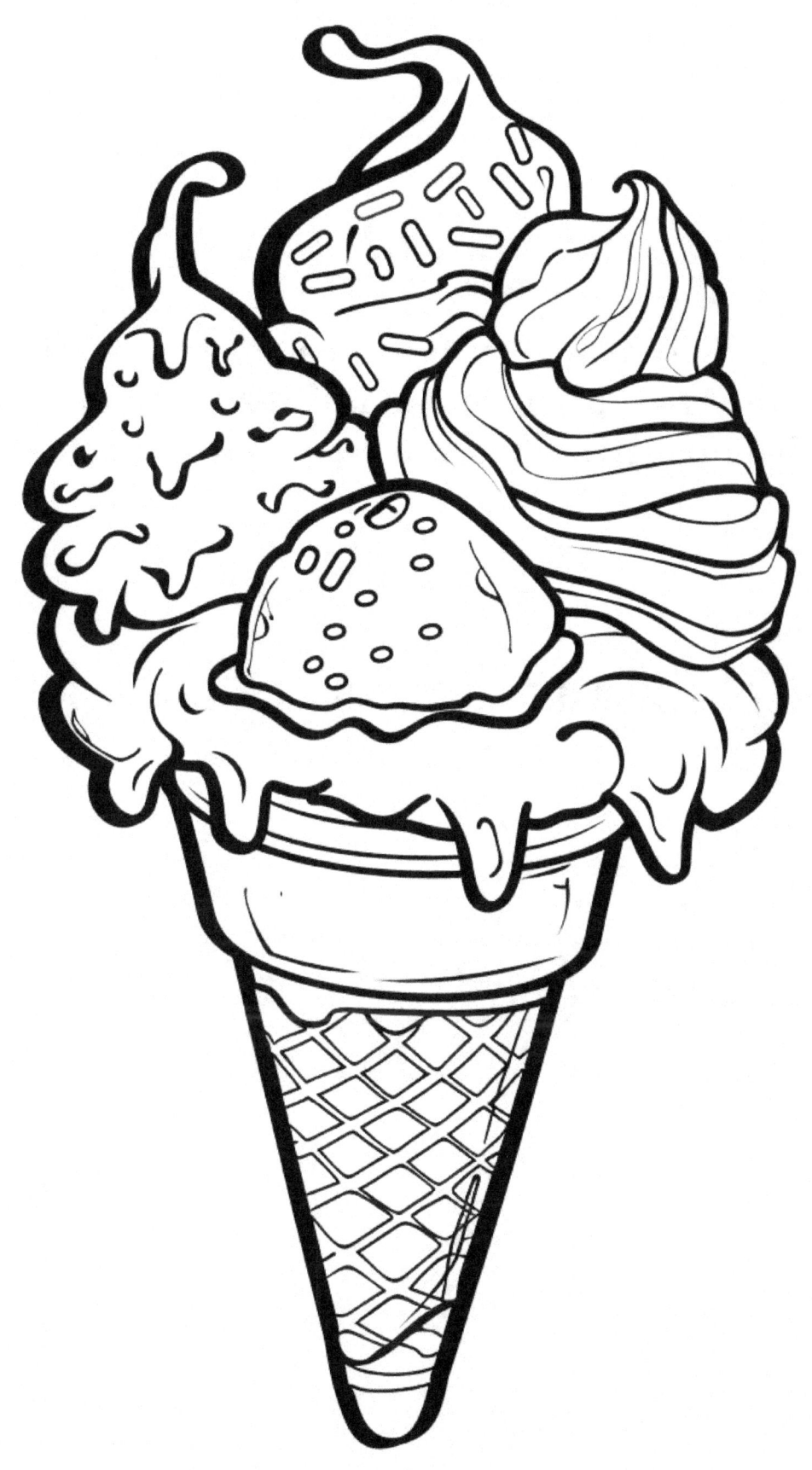

The first known ice cream cone was created at the 1904 World's Fair in St. Louis, Missouri, when an ice cream vendor ran out of cups and rolled up waffles to serve the ice cream instead.

It takes an average of 50 licks to finish a single scoop ice cream cone.

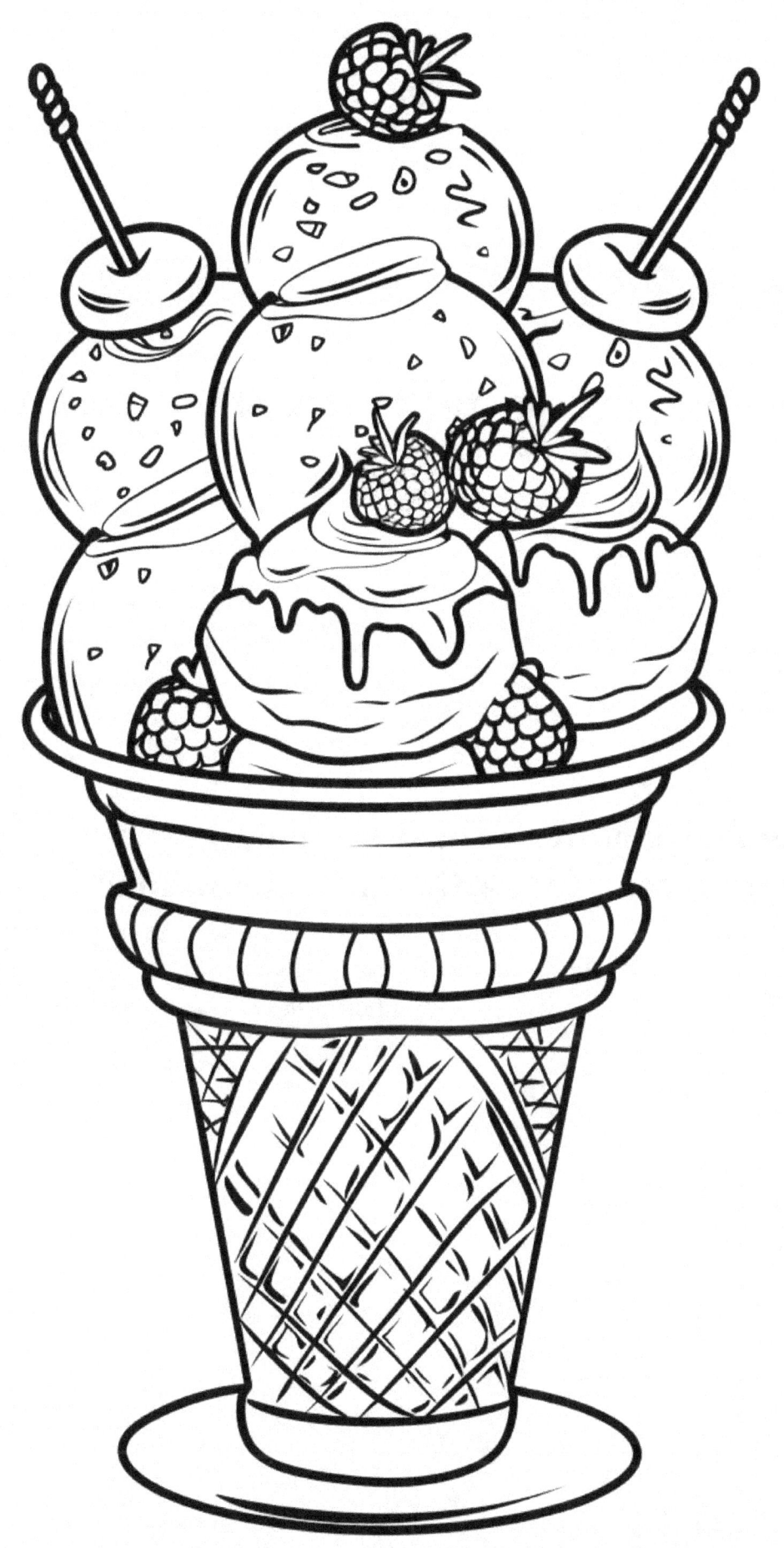

The Guinness World Record for the largest cupcake ever made weighed over 1,200 pounds!

Cupcakes come in countless flavors and decorations, making them a favorite dessert for parties and celebrations.

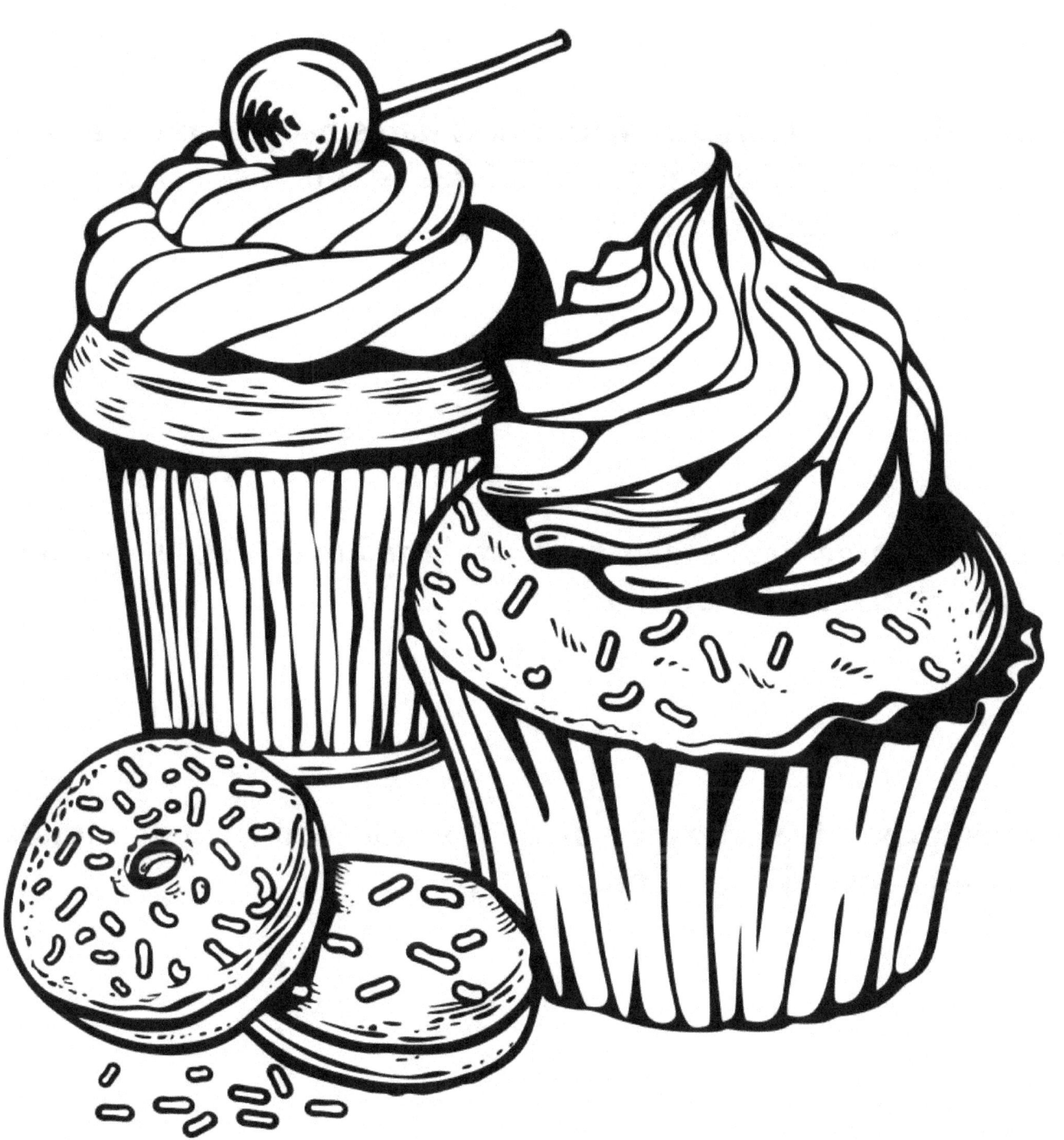

The tradition of celebrating with cakes dates back to ancient civilizations like the Egyptians and Greeks, who used them for religious ceremonies and celebrations.

The world's largest cake ever made weighed over 128,000 pounds and was created in the United States in 2004

The most expensive cake ever made was adorned with diamonds and priced at over $75 million.

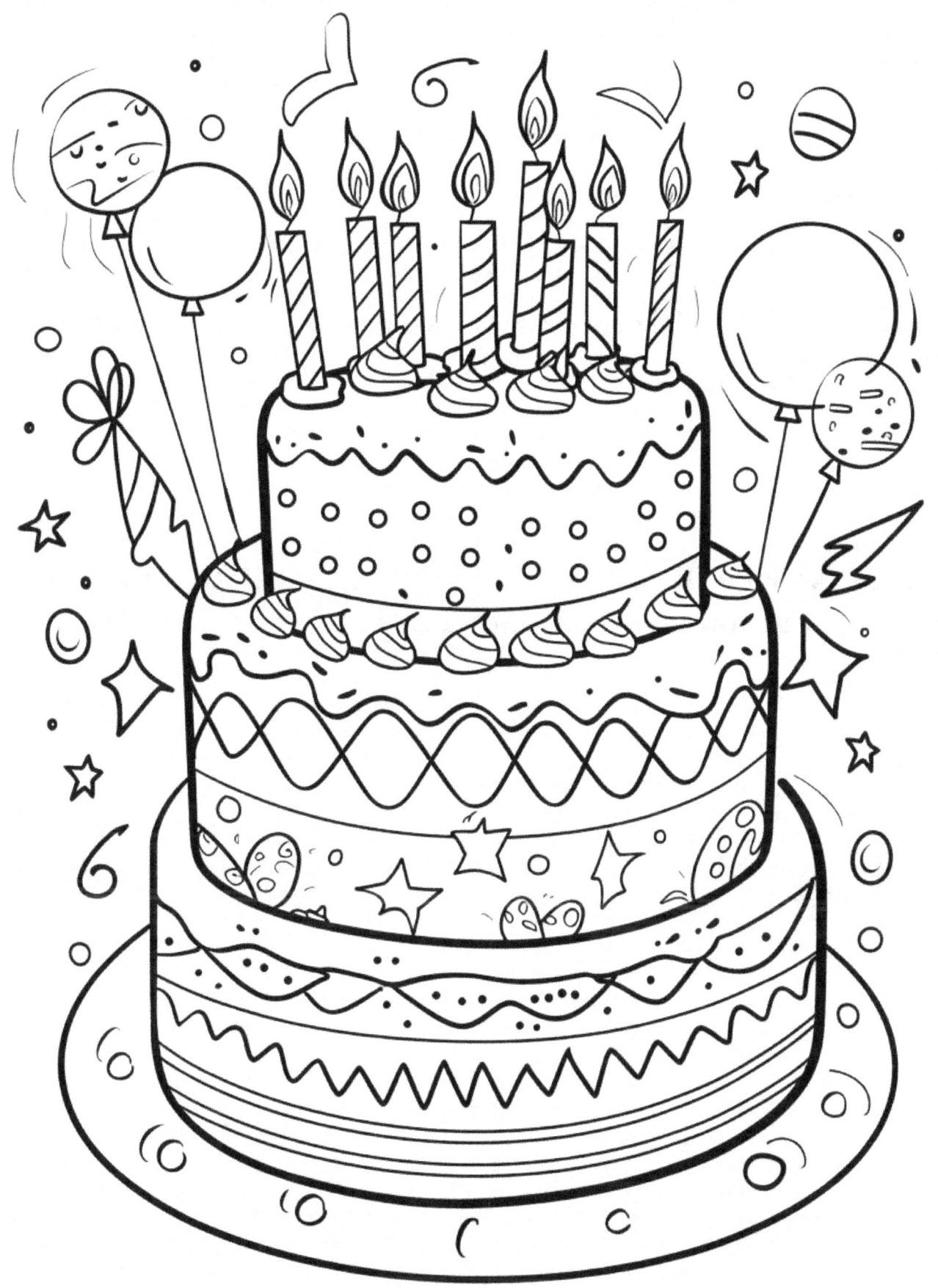

The Guinness World Record for the largest milkshake was set in 2000 and weighed over 6,000 pounds.

Classic milkshake flavors include vanilla, chocolate, and strawberry, but countless variations and flavors exist today.

Orange juice is made by squeezing and extracting the juice from oranges.

The first orange juice machine was patented in the United States in 1910.

Orange juice is rich in vitamin C, potassium, and other essential nutrients.

Freshly squeezed orange juice is often preferred over packaged juice for its superior taste and nutritional value.

Orange juice is a popular breakfast beverage and is also used in cocktails, smoothies, and cooking.

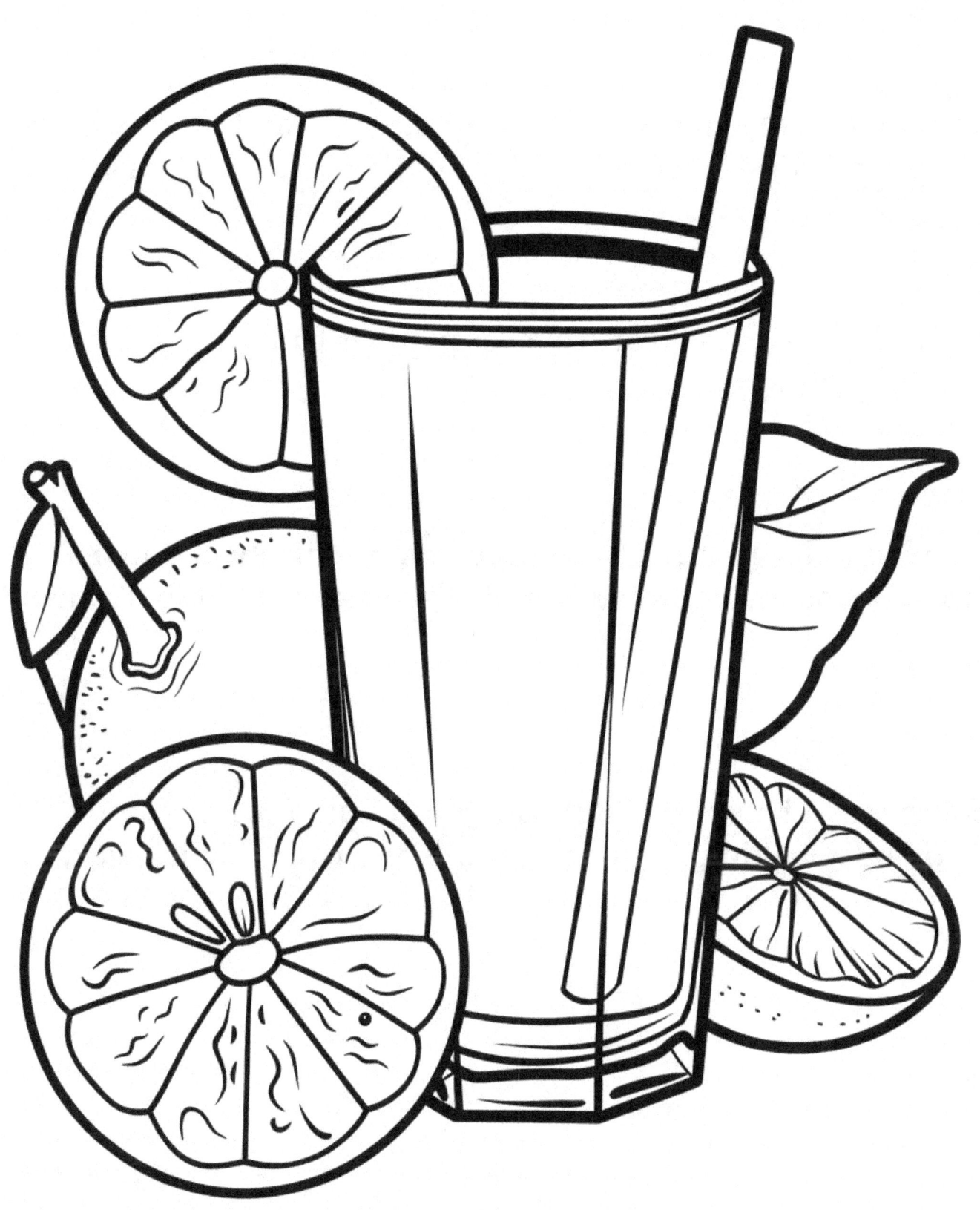

The banana plant is not a tree but a giant herb, and the "trunk" is actually a pseudostem composed of tightly packed leaf bases.

Bananas are one of the world's most popular fruits and are grown in over 135 countries.

The Cavendish banana is the most common variety of banana consumed worldwide, accounting for about 95% of global banana exports.

Bananas are rich in potassium, vitamins C and B6, fiber, and antioxidants, making them a nutritious and convenient snack.

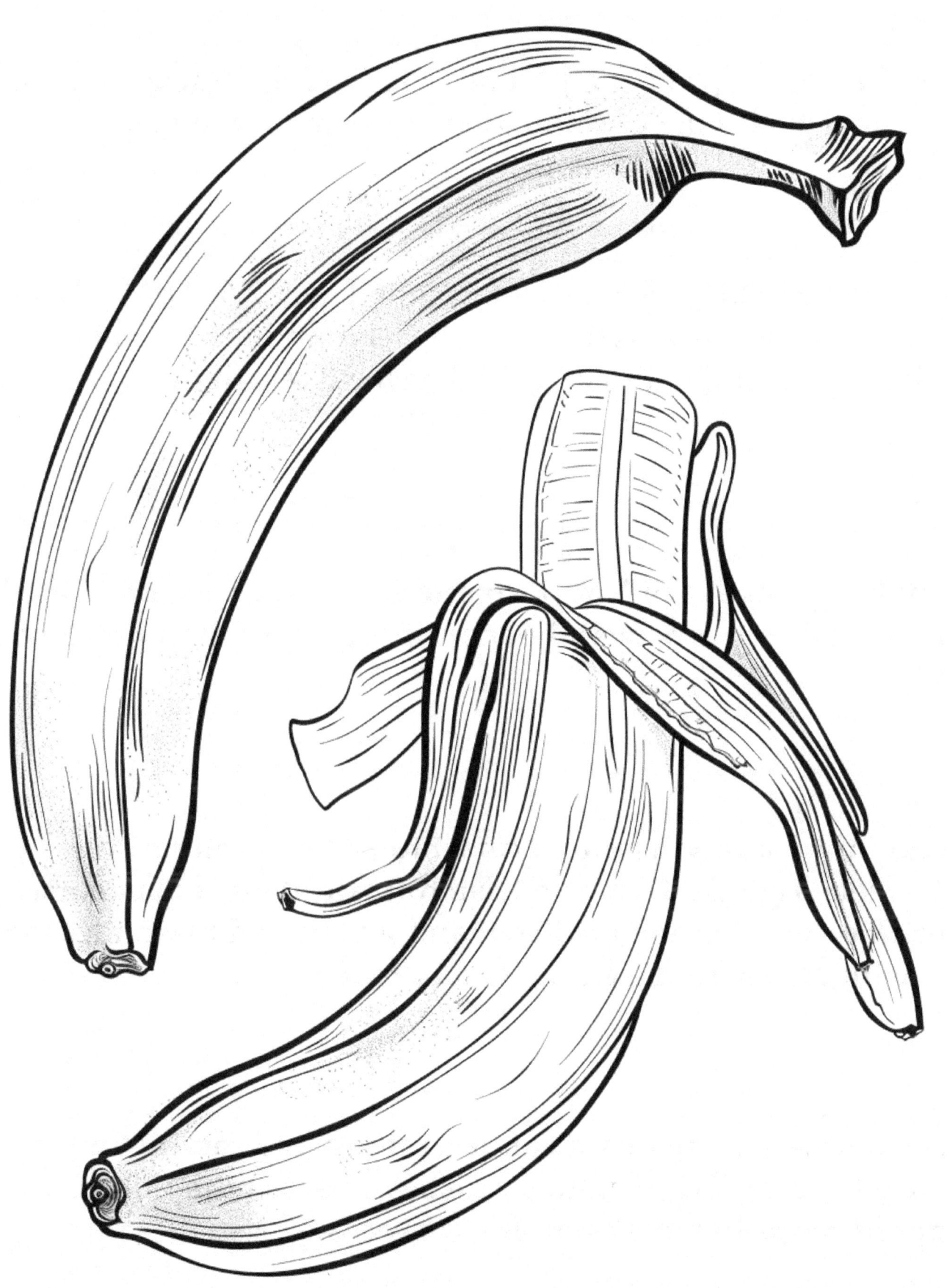

Pumpkins are a type of squash and belong to the Cucurbitaceae family, which also includes cucumbers, melons, and gourds.

The largest pumpkin ever grown weighed over 2,600 pounds and was grown by Mathias Willemijns of Belgium in 2016. This massive pumpkin broke the previous world record by over 300 pounds!

Pumpkins are native to North America and have been cultivated for thousands of years by indigenous peoples for their nutritious seeds and flesh.

The tradition of carving pumpkins into Jack-o'-lanterns for Halloween originated from an Irish folktale about a man named Stingy Jack who tricked the Devil and was cursed to wander the earth with only a hollowed-out turnip to light his way.

Pumpkins are not only used for decorations and carving but are also used in a variety of culinary dishes such as pumpkin pie, pumpkin soup, and roasted pumpkin seeds.

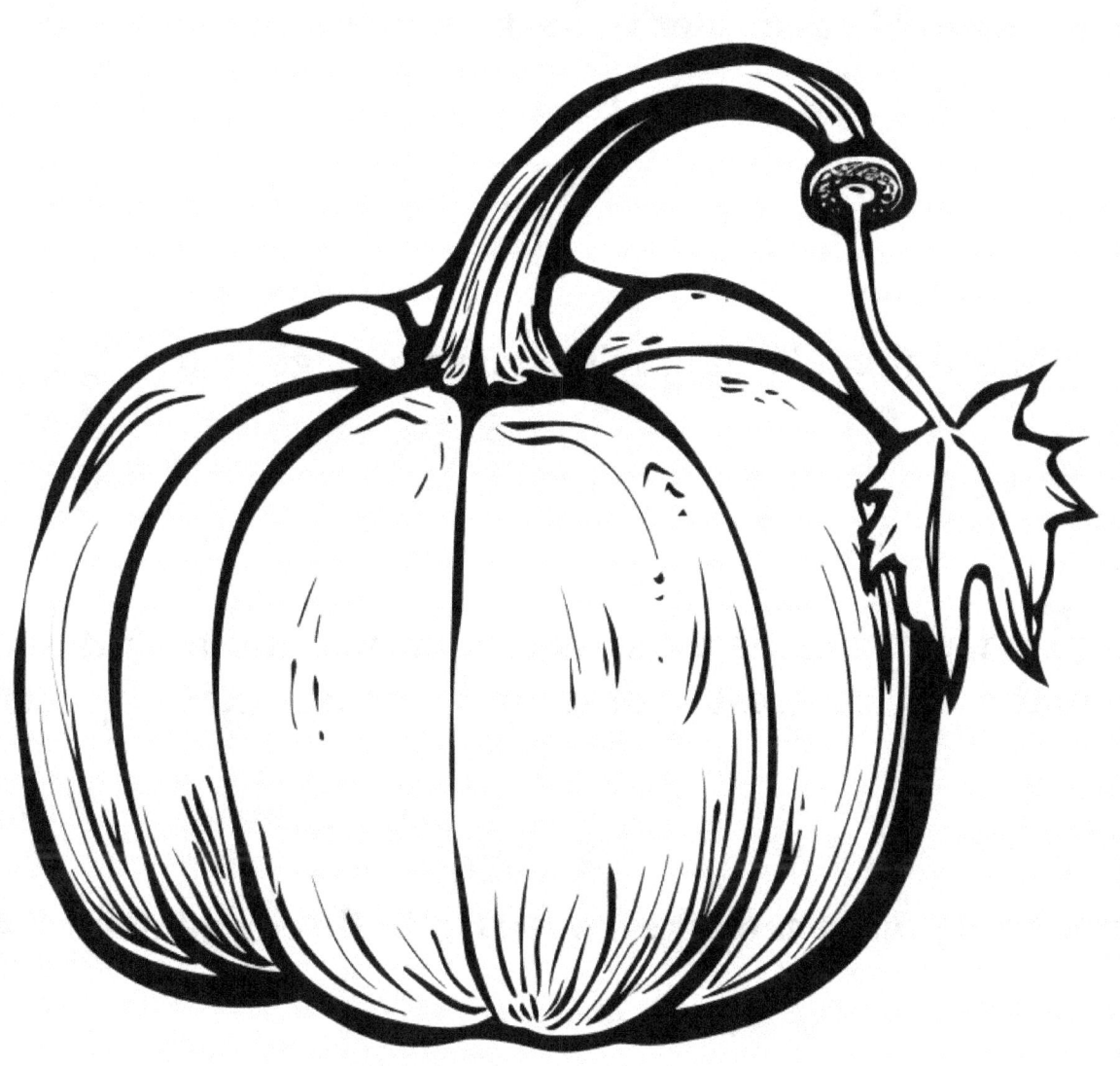

Pineapples were originally native to South America, particularly Brazil and Paraguay.

The first recorded encounter with pineapples by Europeans occurred

during Christopher Columbus's second voyage to the Americas in 1493.

Pineapples were considered a symbol of hospitality and luxury in colonial America because of their rarity and exotic appearance.

The pineapple plant can take up to two to three years to produce fruit.

Pineapples contain bromelain, an enzyme that can tenderize meat and is often used in marinades.

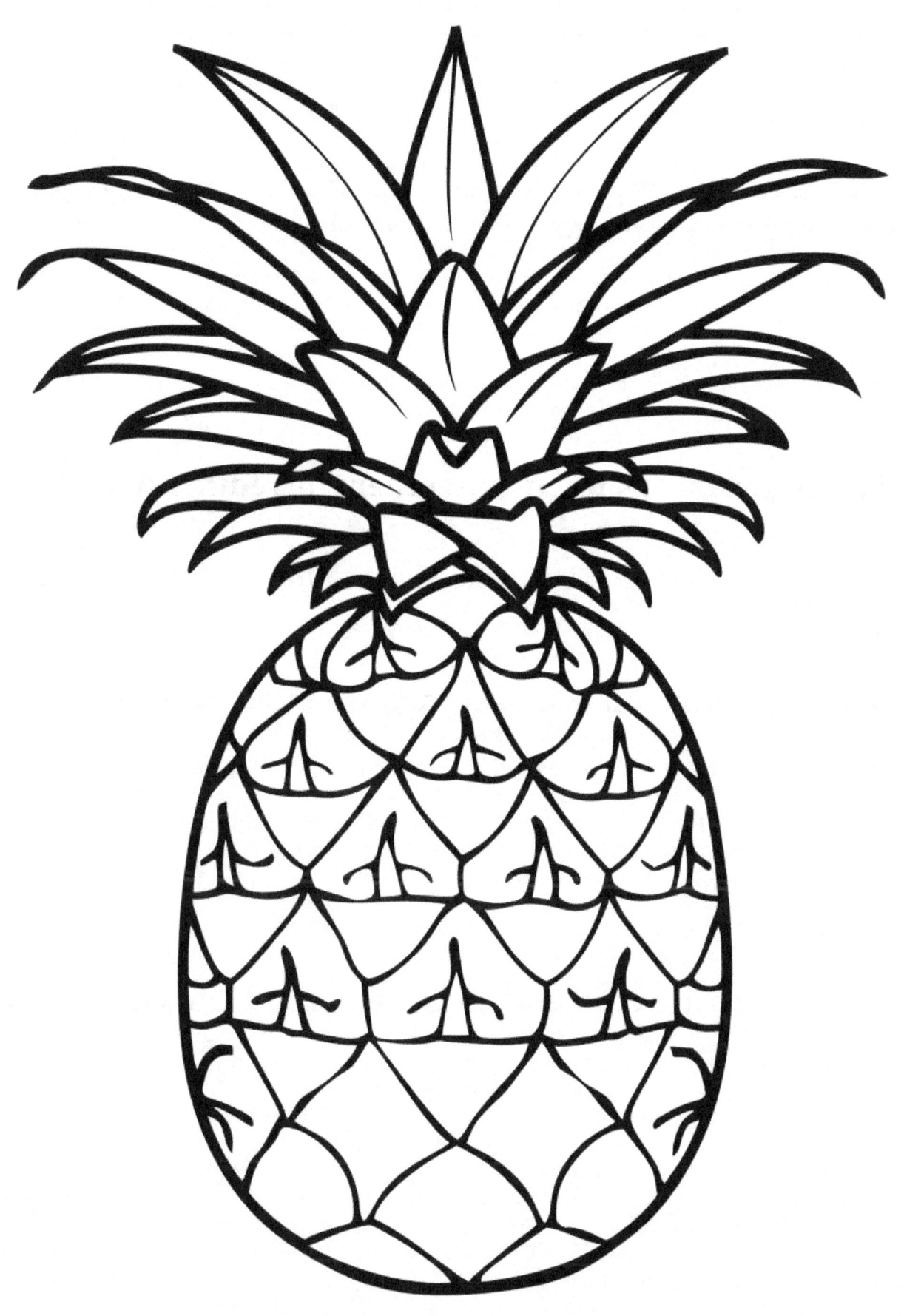

Watermelons are believed to have originated in Africa, possibly in the Kalahari Desert region

Watermelons are 92% water, making them incredibly hydrating fruits.

The heaviest watermelon ever recorded weighed over 350 pounds!

Watermelon seeds are edible and can be roasted and seasoned as a snack.

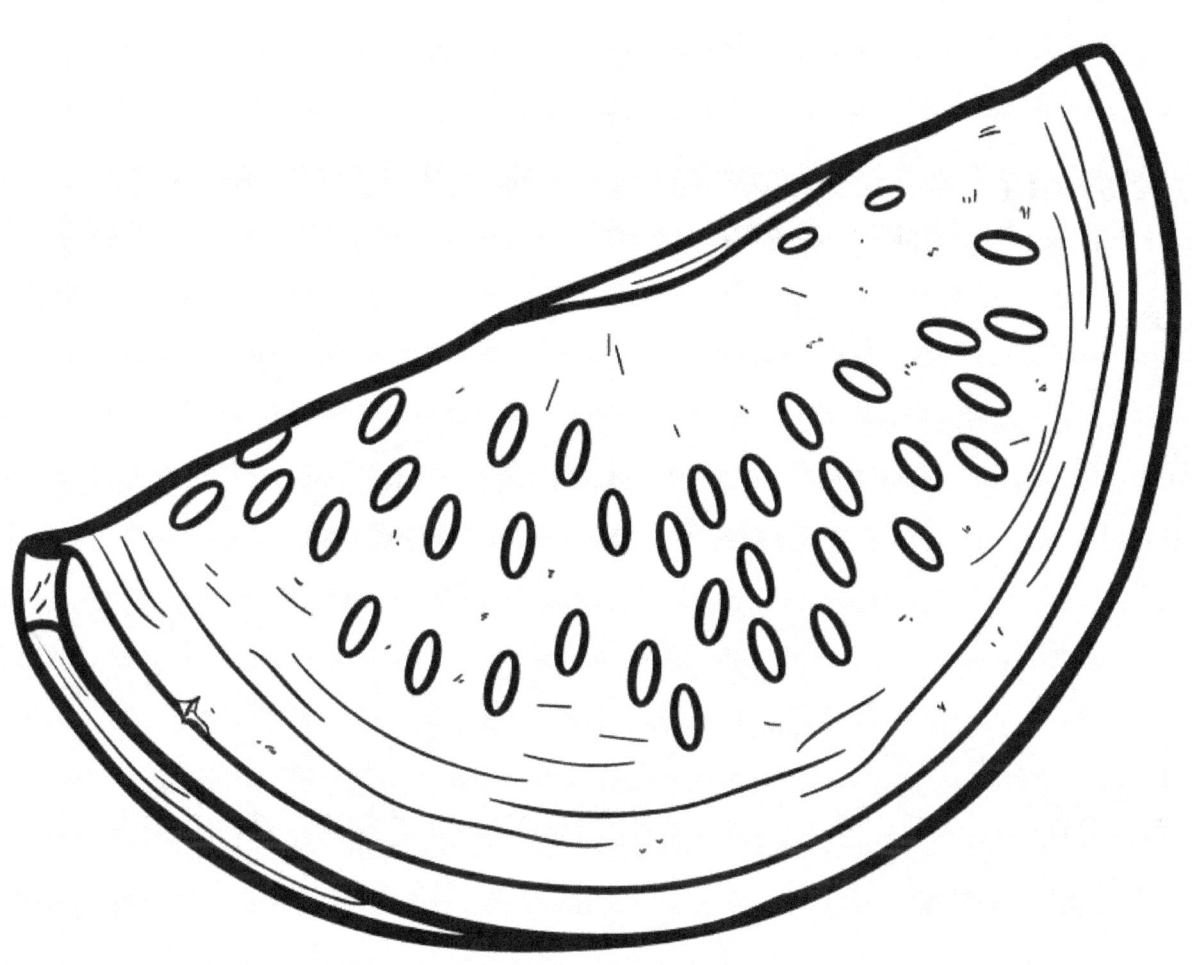

Red wine is made from dark-colored grape varieties and gets its color from the grape skins during fermentation.

The health benefits of red wine include antioxidants and potential heart health benefits when consumed in moderation.

The color of red wine can range from light ruby to deep purple, depending on the grape variety and winemaking process.

Cabernet Sauvignon, Merlot, and Pinot Noir are popular red wine grape varieties.

The temperature at which red wine is served can greatly affect its flavor profile and enjoyment.

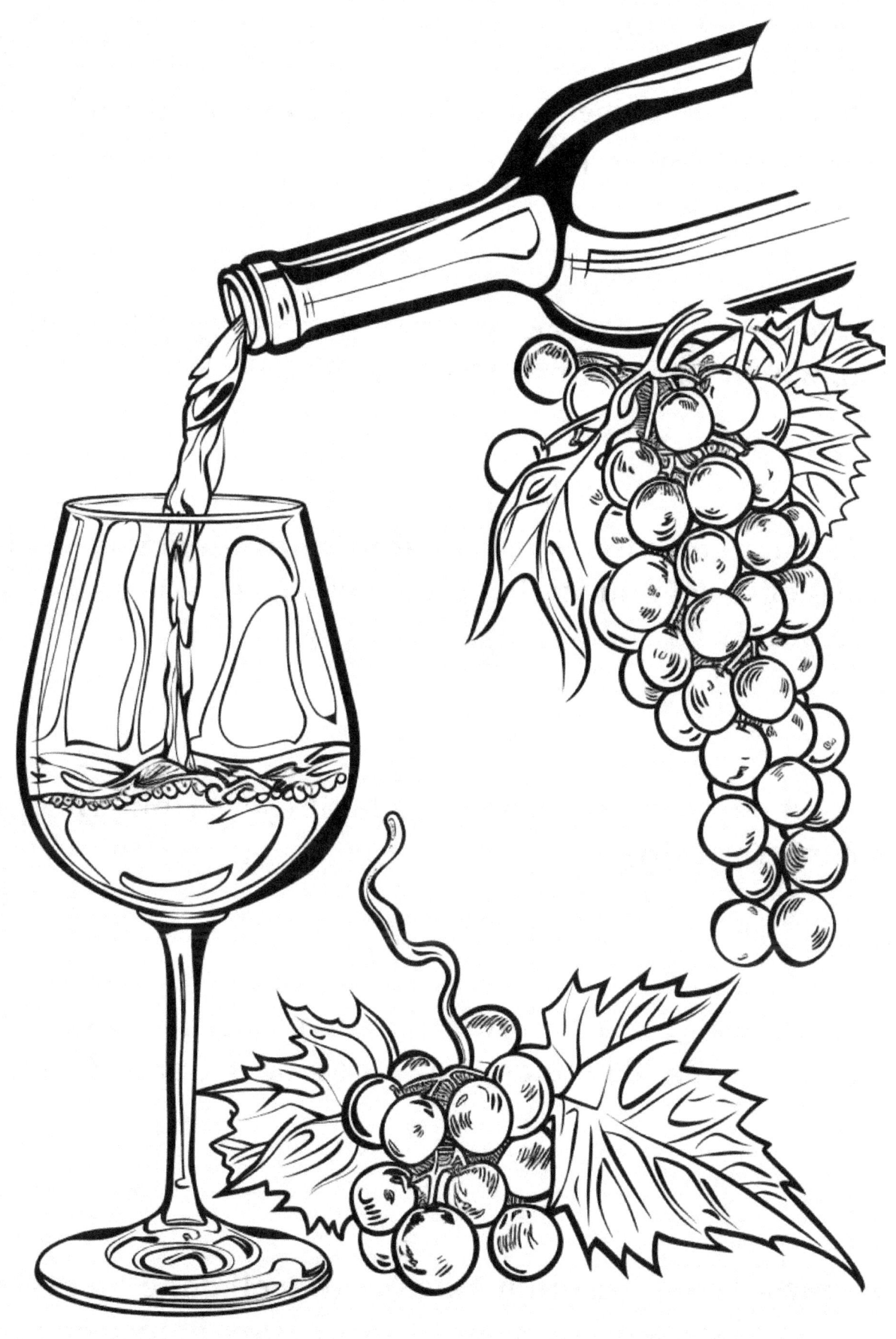

The term "steak" comes from the Old Norse word "steik," which means "to roast on a spit."

The most expensive steak ever sold was a Wagyu beef steak from Japan, which was auctioned for over $3,000!

The Maillard reaction is responsible for the delicious browning and flavor development that occurs when steak is cooked at high temperatures.

The most popular steak cuts include ribeye, sirloin, filet mignon, and New York strip.

The Guinness World Record for the largest steak ever cooked weighed over 3,000 pounds and was made in South Africa in 2014.

The phrase "rare," "medium rare," and "well done" to describe the doneness of steak originated in 17th-century French culinary culture

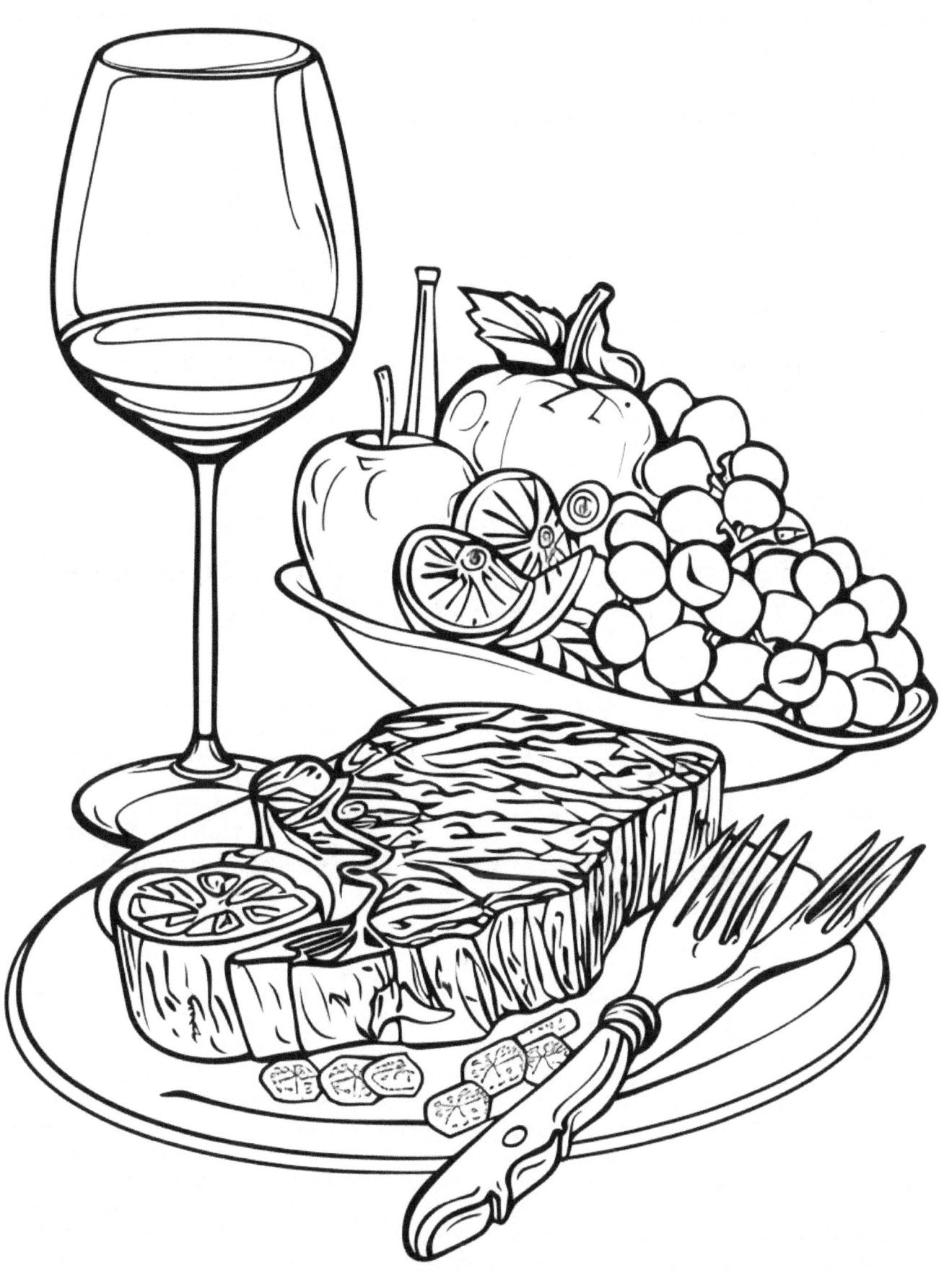

The word "candy" comes from the Arabic word "qandi," which means "sugar."

The first candies were made from honey mixed with various fruits and nuts by ancient civilizations like the Egyptians and Greeks.

The world's largest candy store, Dylan's Candy Bar, is located in New York City and covers over 15,000 square feet.

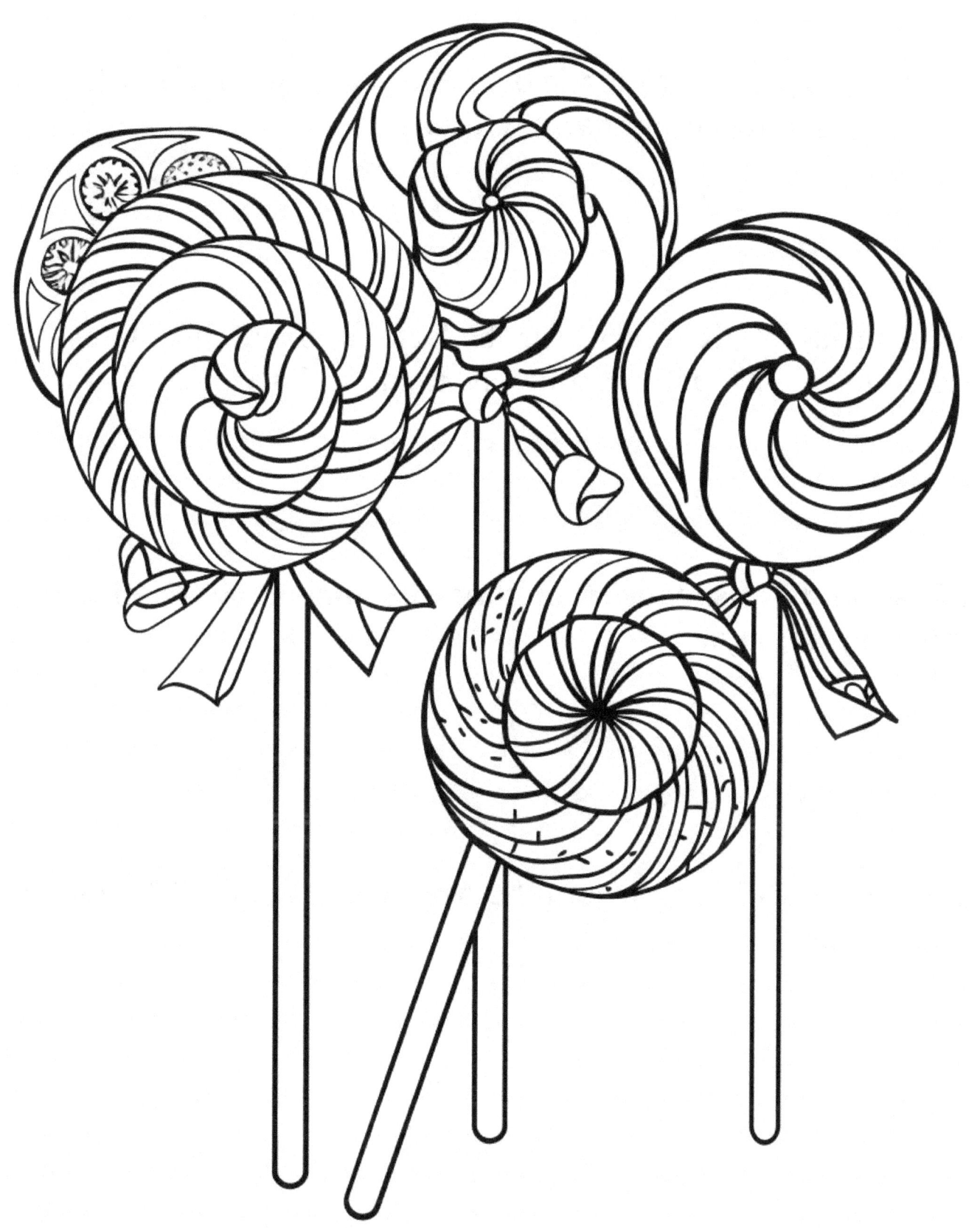

The first candy cane was made over 350 years ago in Germany and was originally straight and white.

The Guinness World Record for the largest box of chocolates weighed over 5,000 pounds and was made in Italy in 2017.

The first candy was made from honey by ancient civilizations over 6,000 years ago.

The word "candy" comes from the Arabic word "qandi," which means "sugar

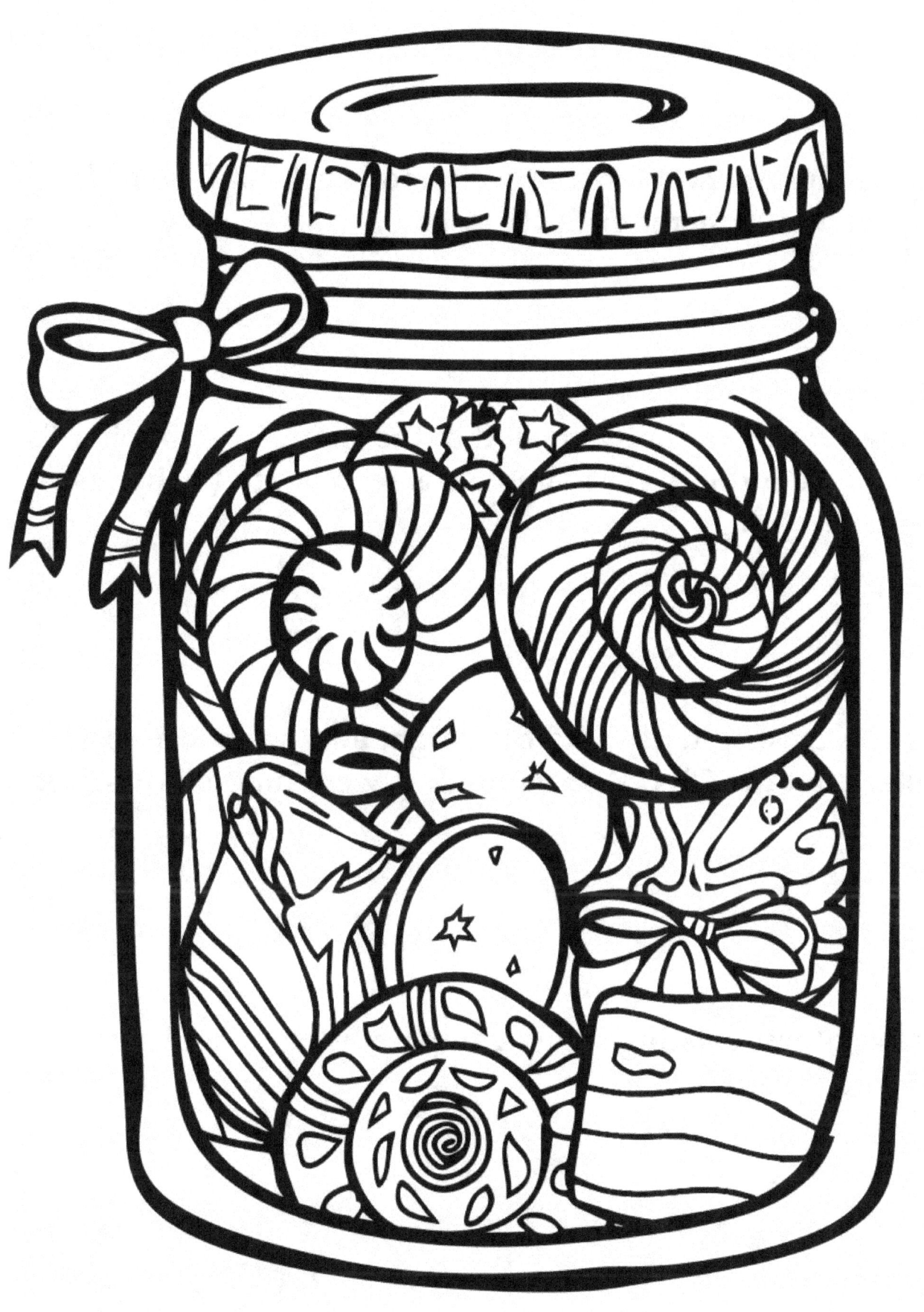

The world's largest chocolate bar weighed over 12,770 pounds and was made in Armenia in 2010.

Candy canes were originally created in the shape of a shepherd's crook to represent the staff of shepherds who visited baby Jesus in Bethlehem.

Jelly beans were originally sold by weight and became associated with Easter after the Civil War when they were marketed as "egg-shaped."

The world's oldest existing candy company is Fry's, which was founded in England in 1761.

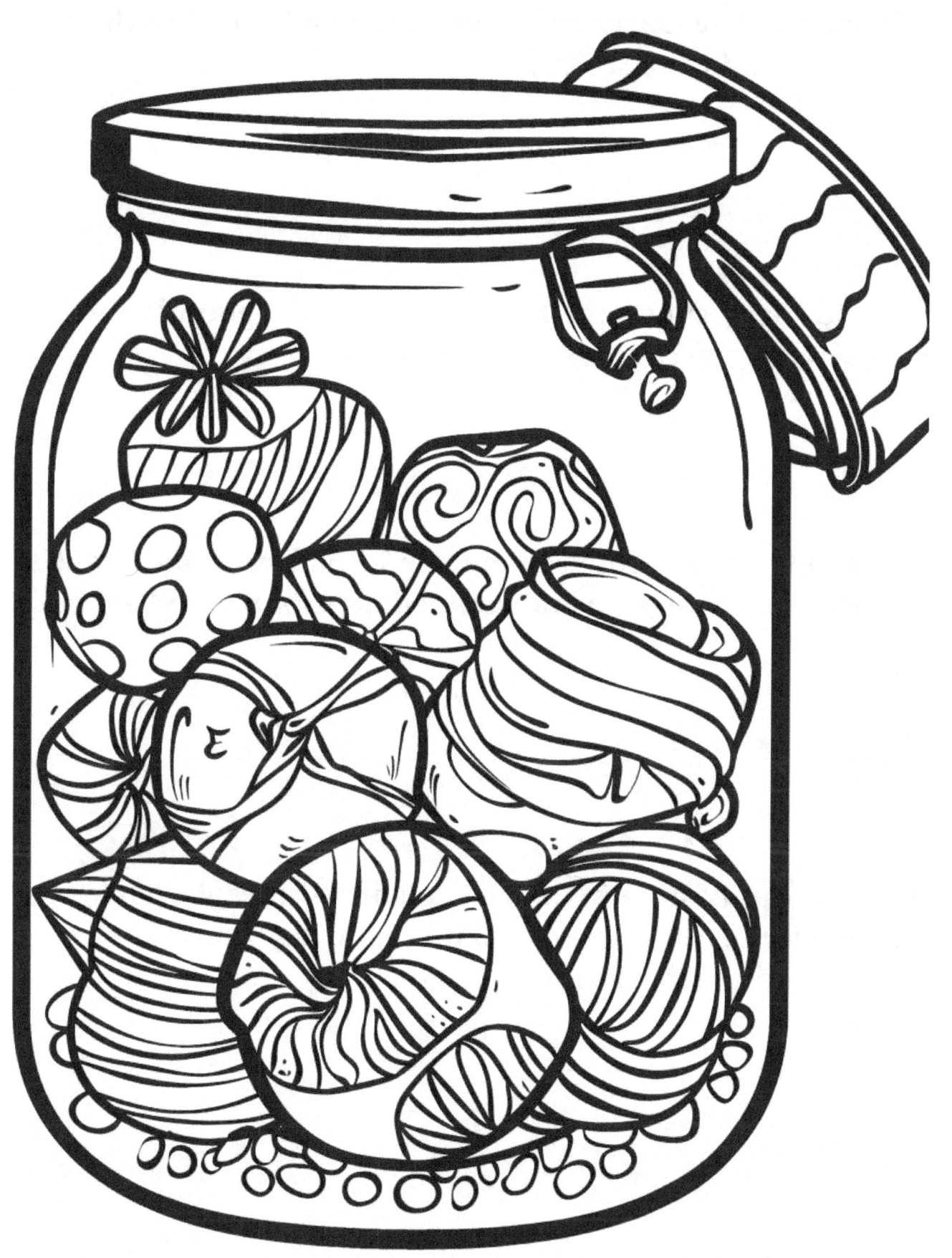

The first chocolate Easter eggs were made in Europe in the early 19th century and were solid.

The world's largest gummy bear weighs over 5 pounds and contains over 6,000 calories!

Cotton candy was invented in the late 19th century by a dentist named William Morrison and confectioner John C. Wharton.

The largest candy store in the world is in Minnesota, USA, covering over 10,000 square feet and featuring thousands of different candies from around the globe.

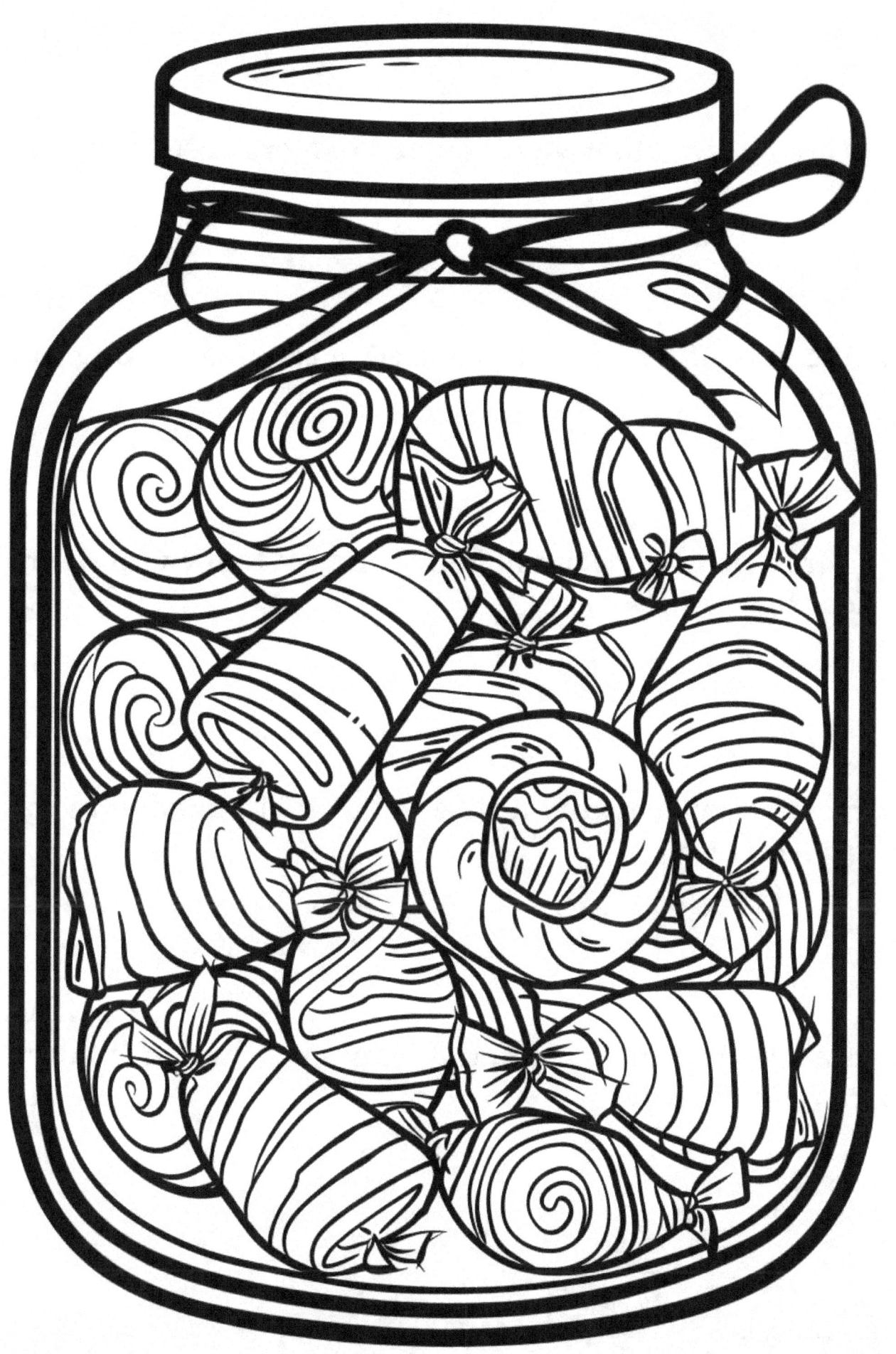

Lemons are believed to have originated in Northeast India and China.

The acidic juice of lemons is often used in cooking, baking, and beverages.

Lemons are a rich source of vitamin C and are known for their antioxidant properties.

The largest lemon ever grown weighed over 11 pounds and was grown in Israel.

Lemons are often used as a natural cleaning agent due to their antibacterial properties

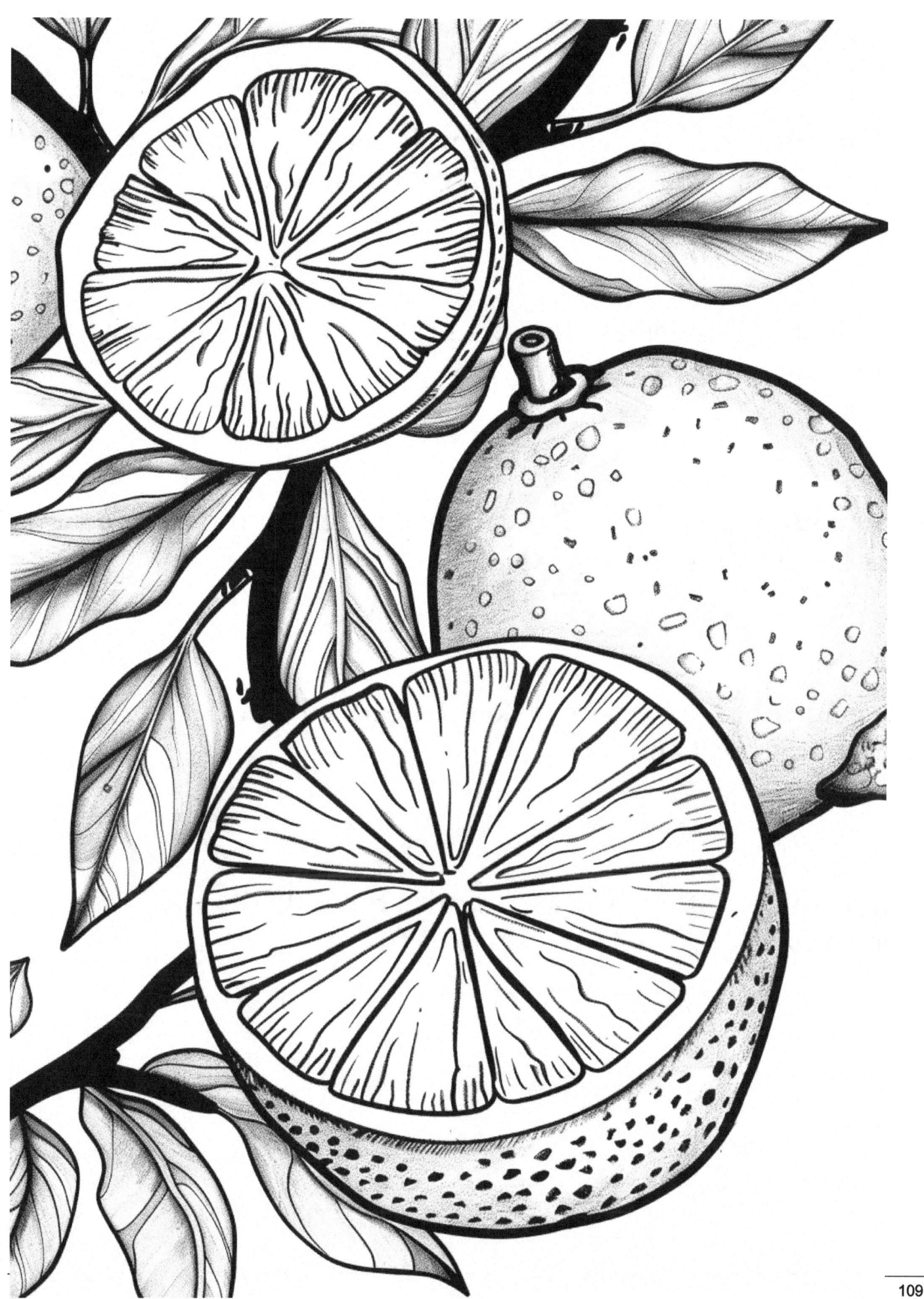

Lemon juice is a popular ingredient in cooking, baking, and beverages, known for its tangy flavor and acidity.

The vitamin C content in lemon juice helps boost the immune system and promotes healthy skin.

Lemon juice can be used as a natural cleaner for surfaces and as a remedy for stains and odors.

The acidity of lemon juice makes it an effective marinade for tenderizing meat and fish.

Lemon juice is often used as a garnish for cocktails and mocktails, adding a refreshing citrus flavo

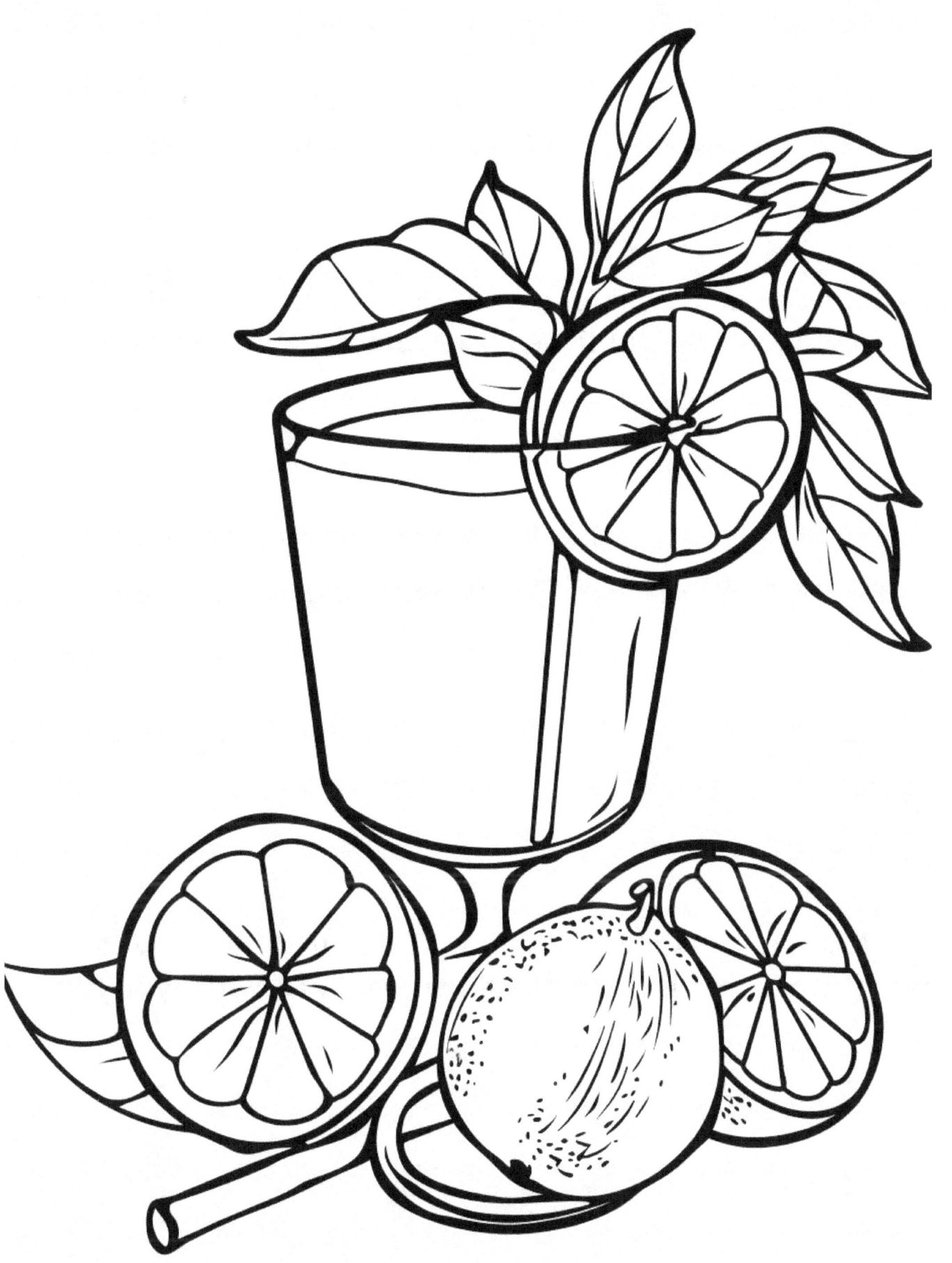

Ice cream is believed to have originated in China around 200 BCE, where it was made by mixing snow with fruit juices.

The first recorded recipe for ice cream in the United States dates back to 1744 and was published by a colonist in Maryland.

The most popular flavor of ice cream in the United States is vanilla, followed by chocolate and strawberry.

The largest ice cream sundae ever made weighed over 24,000 pounds!

July is National Ice Cream Month in the United States, with National Ice Cream Day celebrated on the third Sunday of July.

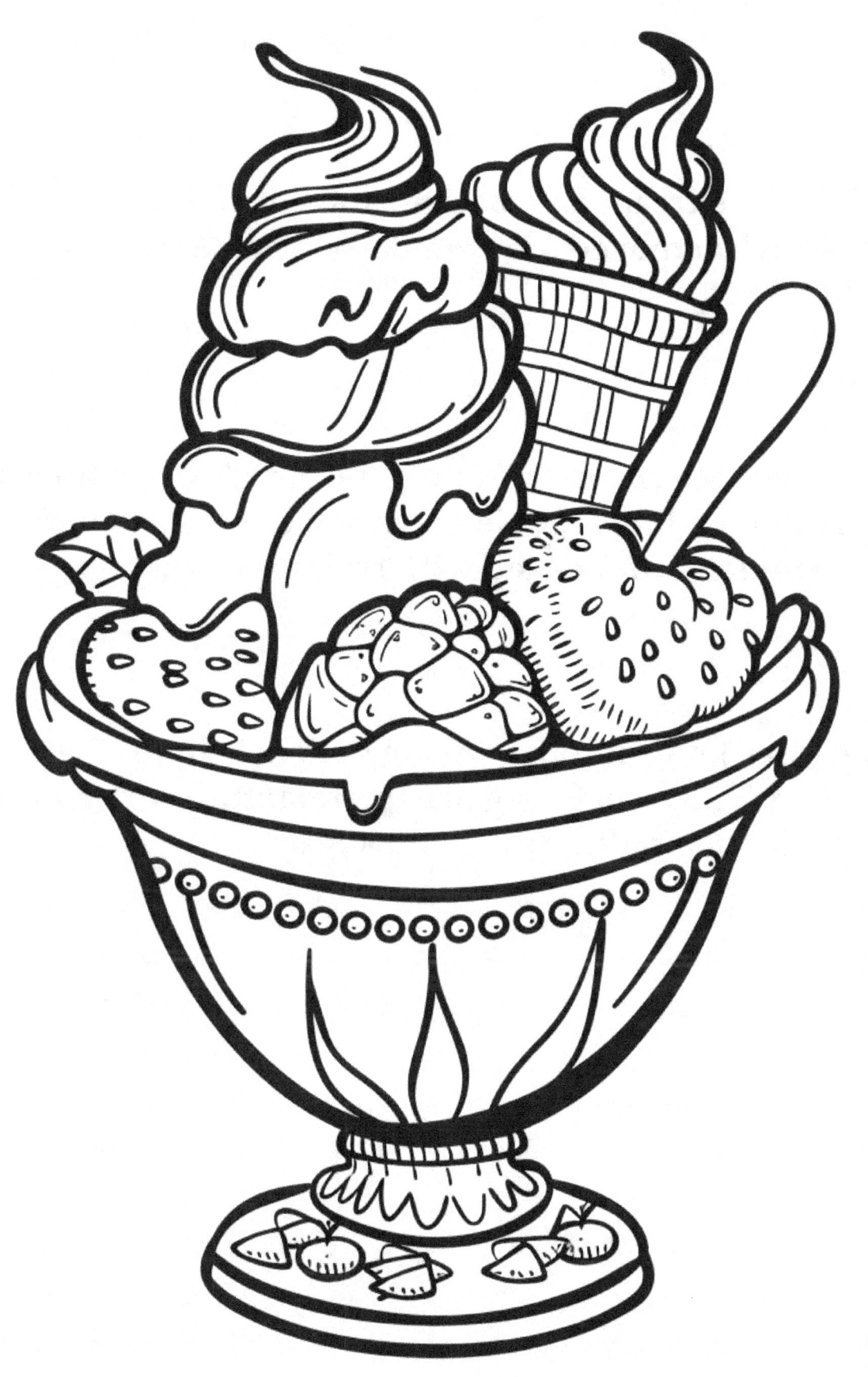

The origins of ice cream date back to ancient civilizations such as the Chinese, who enjoyed a frozen dessert made from snow, fruit juices, and honey.

The first known ice cream recipe was recorded in the 4th century B.C. by the Roman Emperor Nero, who ordered ice to be brought from the mountains and mixed with fruit toppings.

Ice cream as we know it today became popular in the 17th century when Italian chefs began experimenting with frozen desserts made from milk, cream, and sugar.

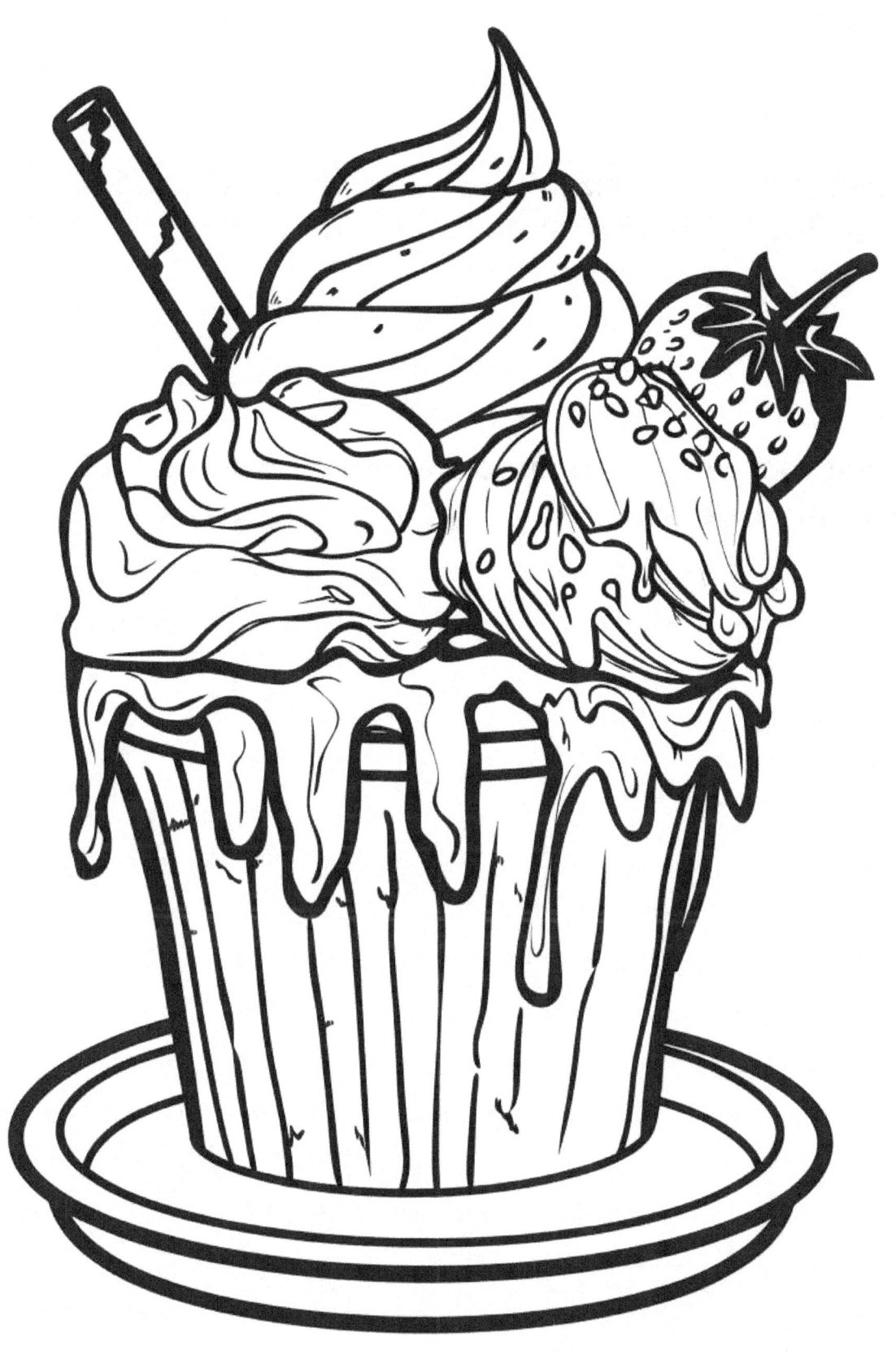

The most popular flavor of ice cream in the United States is vanilla, followed by chocolate and butter pecan.

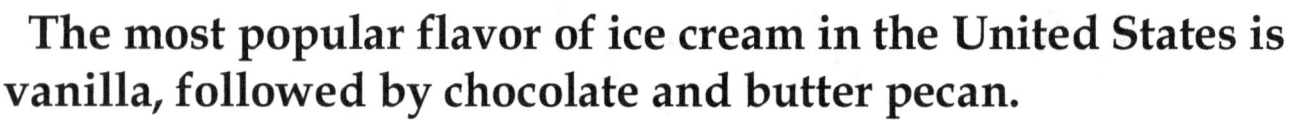

The world's largest ice cream cone was over 10 feet tall and was made in Italy in 2015.

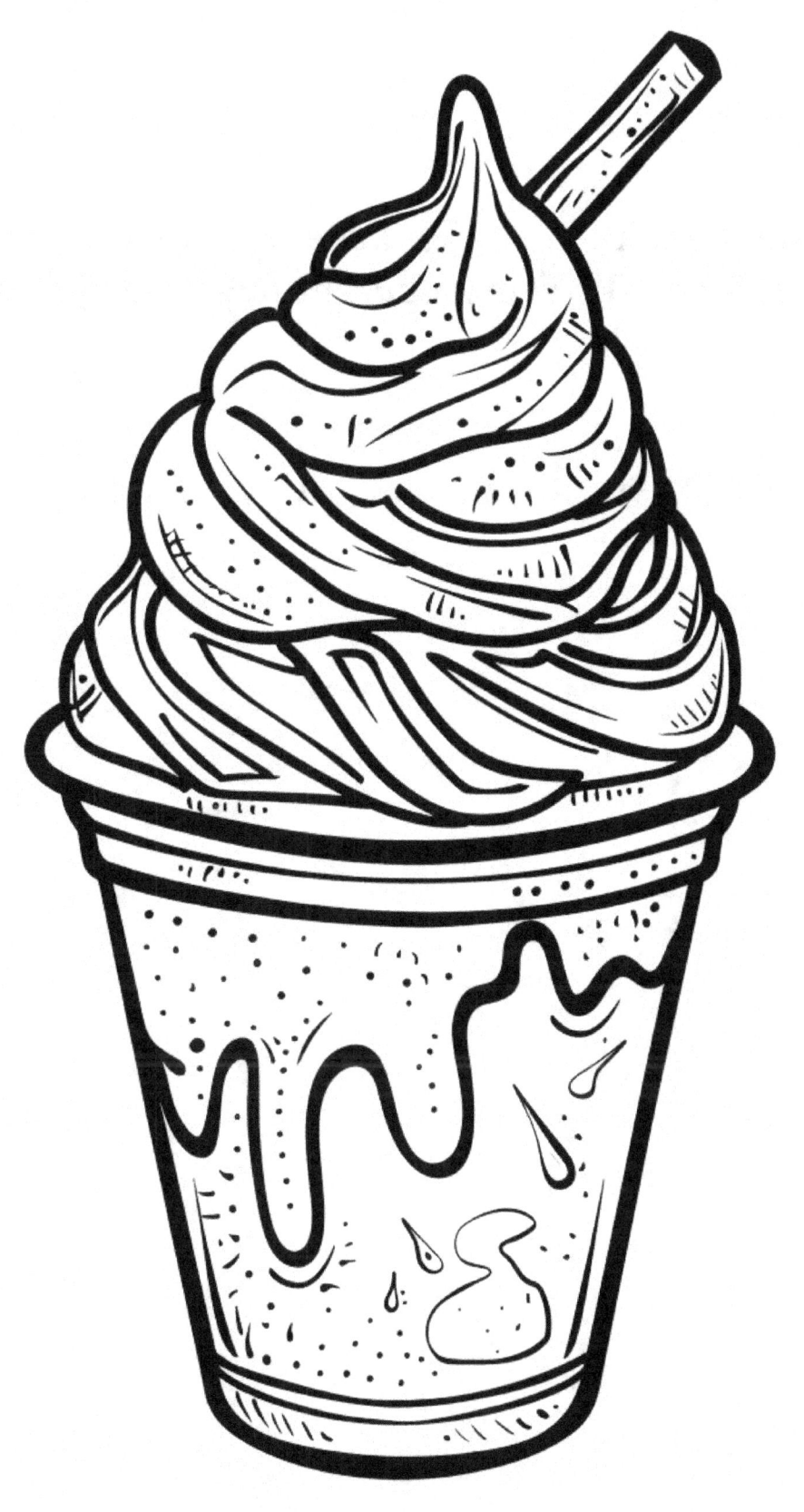

The oldest known recipe for cake dates back to ancient Rome and included ingredients like eggs, flour, honey, and spices.

The Guinness World Record for the tallest cake ever made is over 30 feet tall!

The largest chocolate cake ever made weighed over 50,000 pounds and was created in the United States in 2011.

The world record for the most expensive chocolate cake is $35 million, featuring edible gold leaf and diamonds.

The chocolate cake is one of the most popular desserts worldwide, enjoyed by people of all ages.

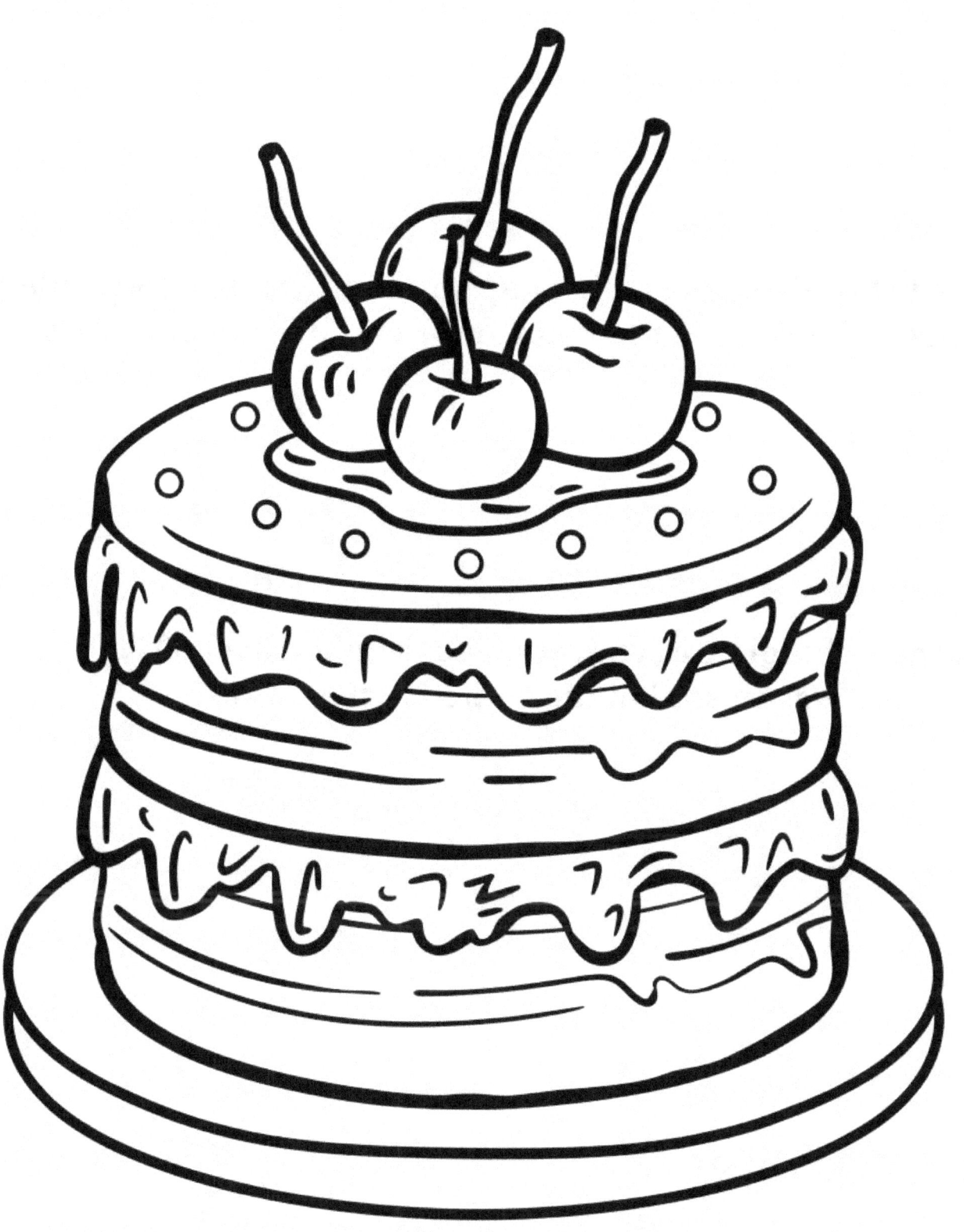

The first chocolate cake recipe appeared in 1764 in a book titled "The Art of Cookery Made Plain and Easy" by Hannah Glasse.

The largest chocolate cake ever made weighed over 50,000 pounds and was created in the United States in 2011.

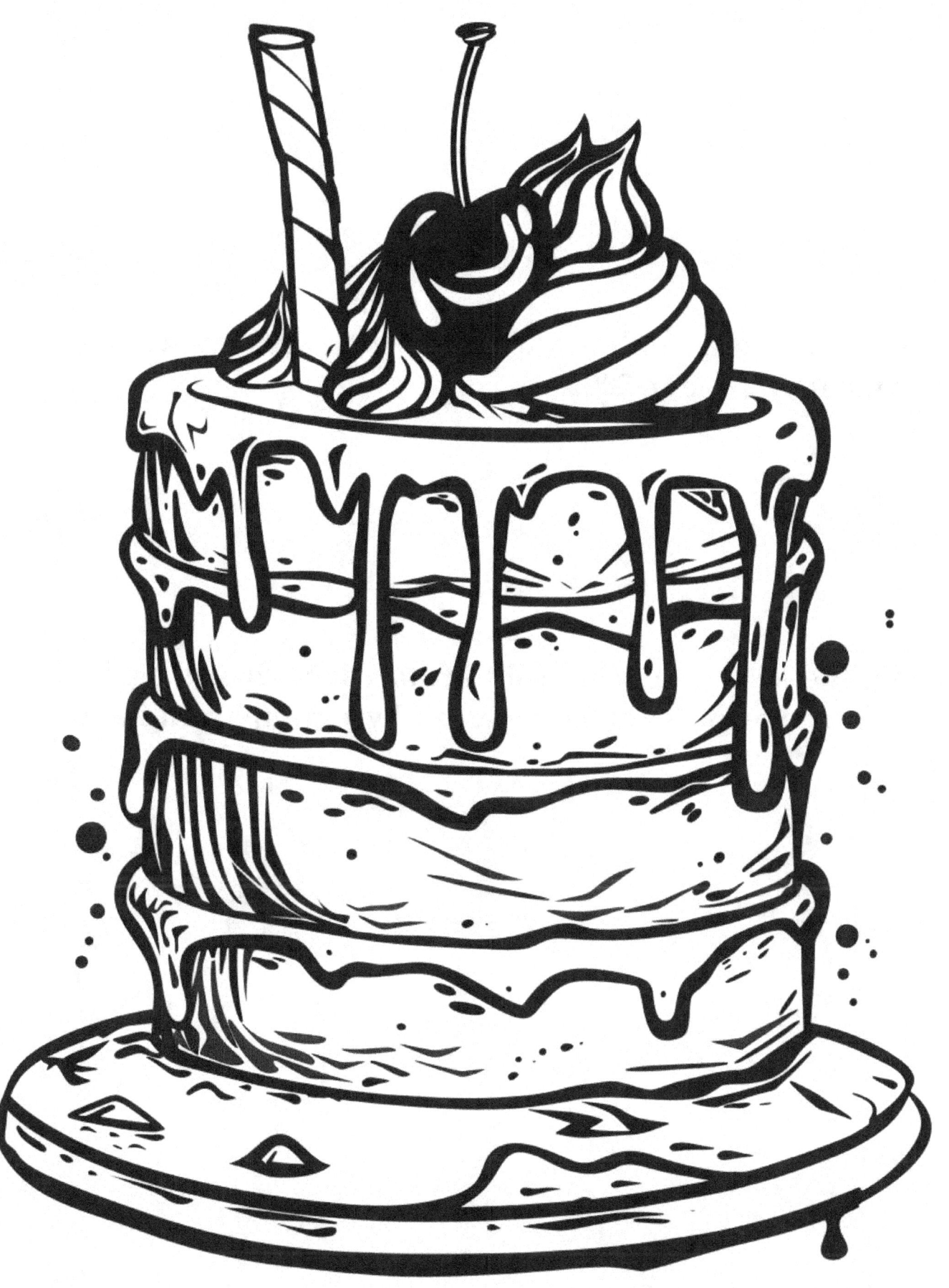

The world's largest sandwich weighed over 5,000 pounds and was made in Mexico in 2005.

The Guinness World Record for the most sandwiches made in one hour by a team is 49,000, achieved by a group in India in 2017.

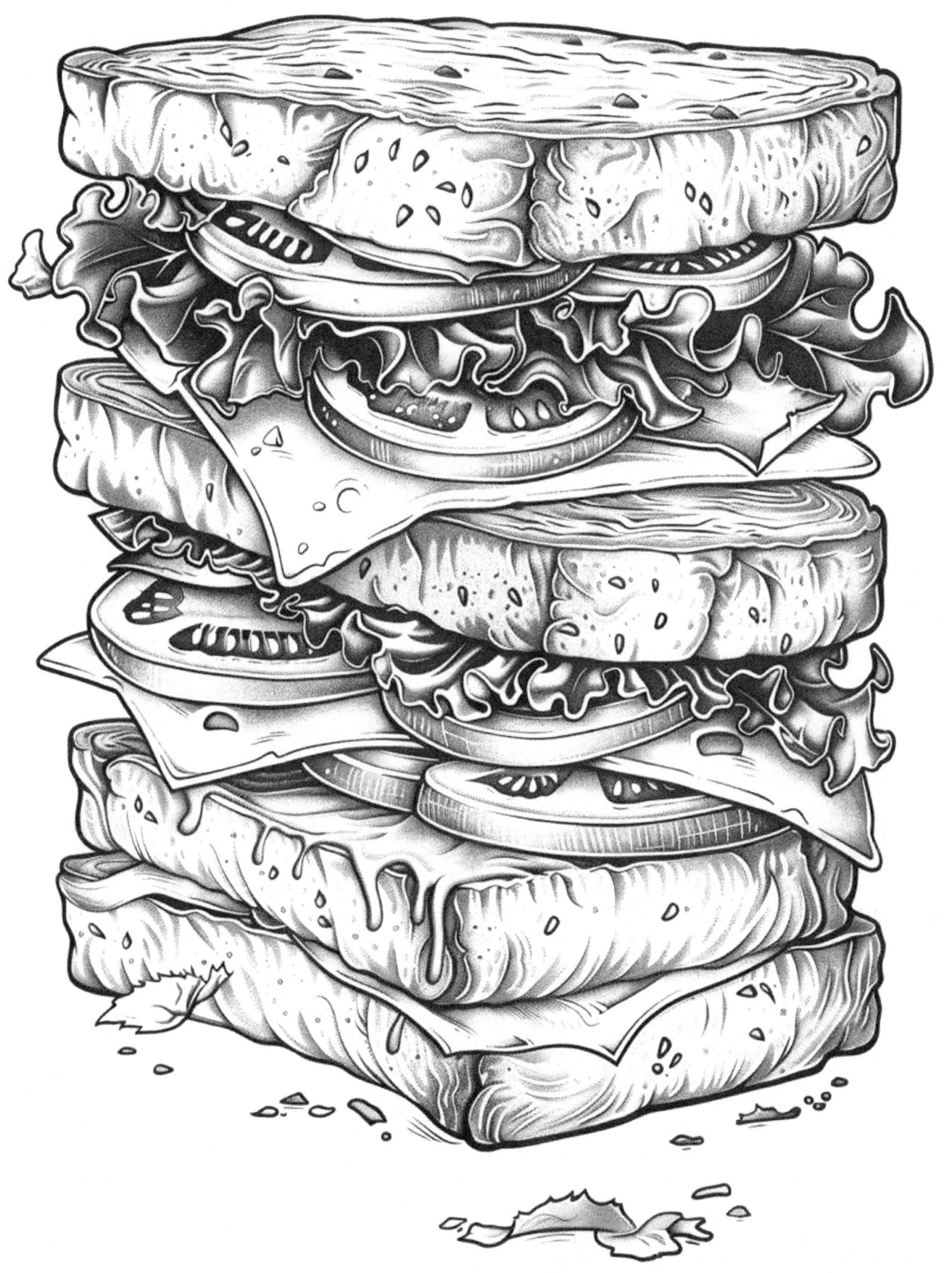

The first donut machine was invented in 1920 by Adolph Levitt, a Russian immigrant living in New York City.

The most popular donut flavors in the United States are glazed, chocolate frosted, and Boston cream.

The world's most expensive donut is the "Luxury Zebra Cro" from Krispy Kreme in the United Kingdom, which is coated in 24-karat gold and edible diamonds and costs over $1,900!

Dunkin' Donuts, now known simply as Dunkin', is one of the largest and most famous donut chains in the world, with over 12,000 locations worldwide.

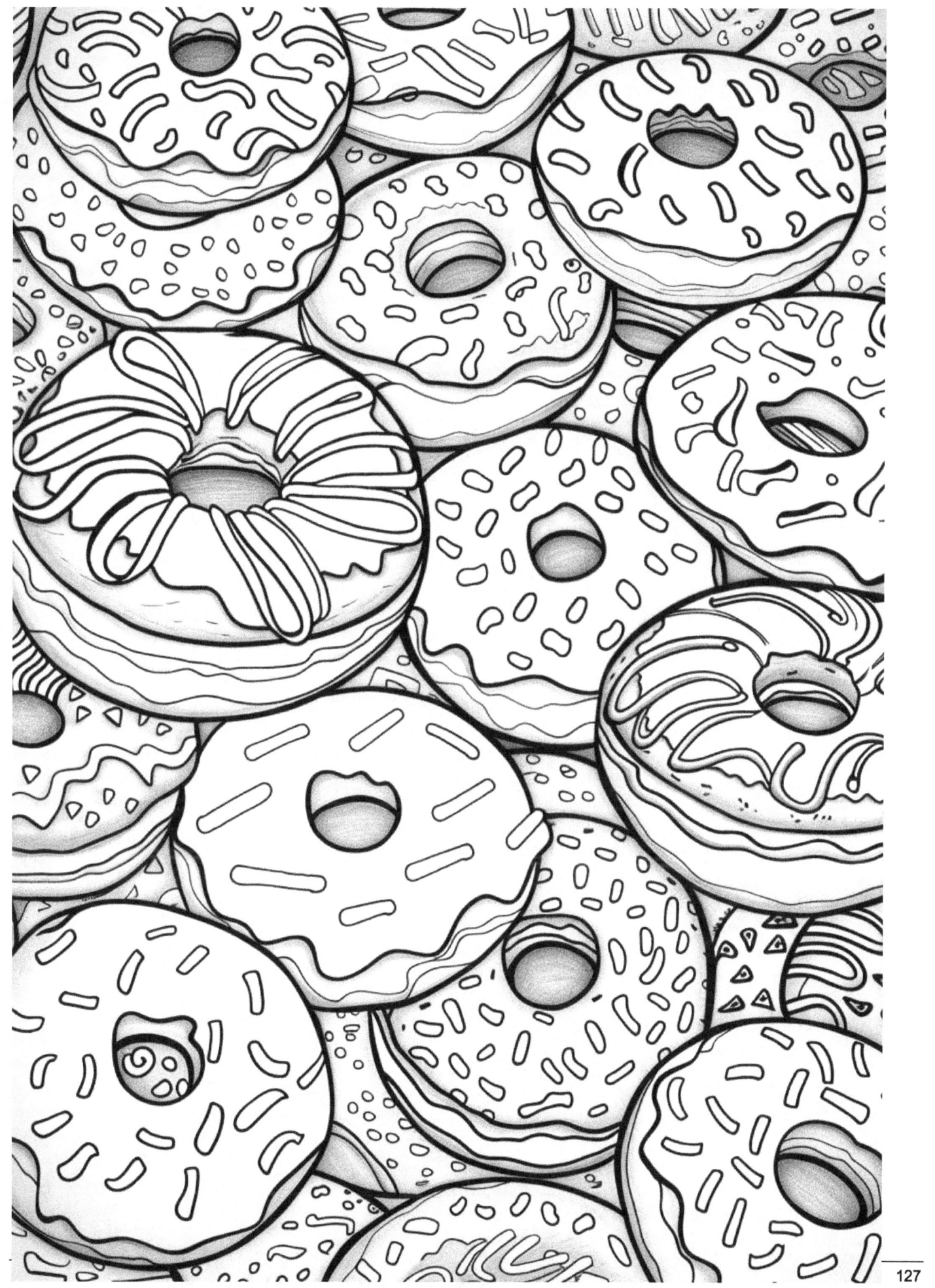

Experiment page

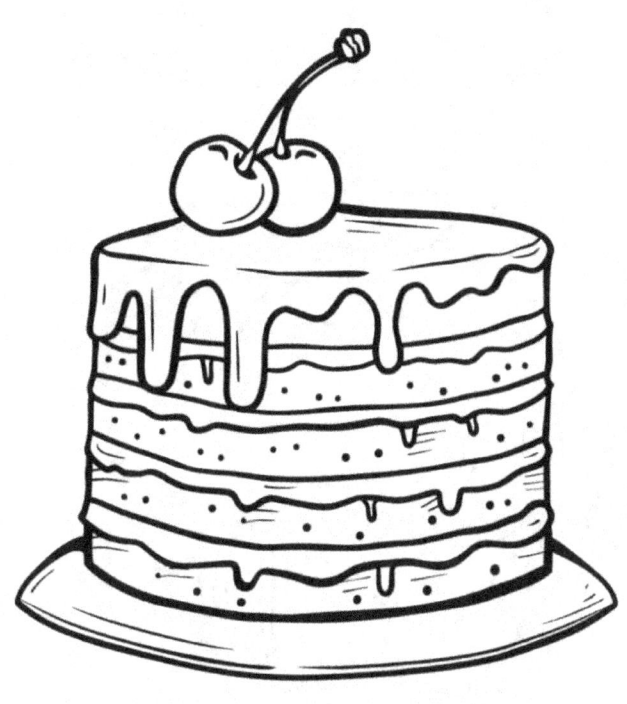
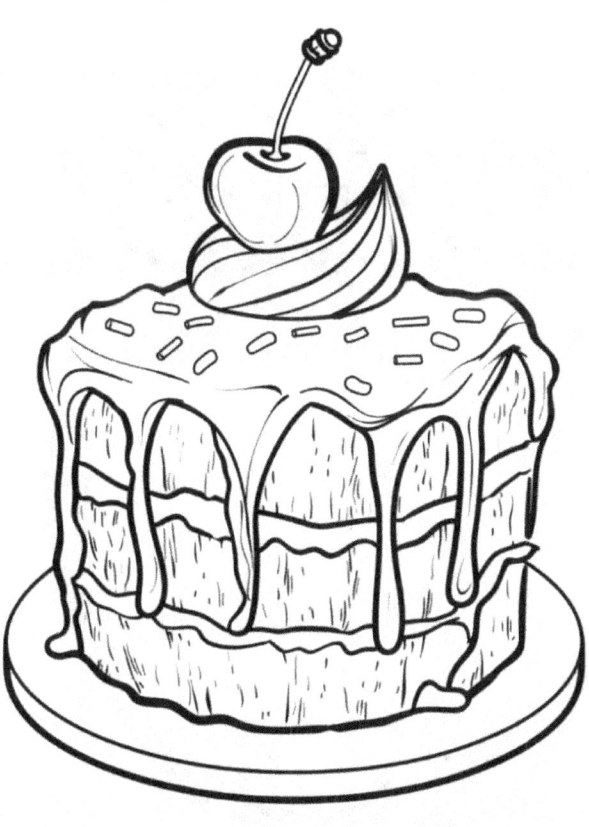
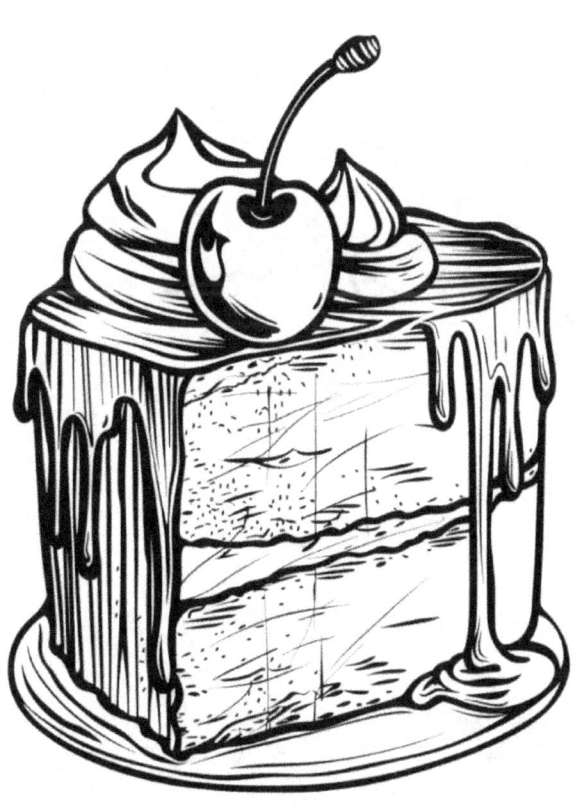

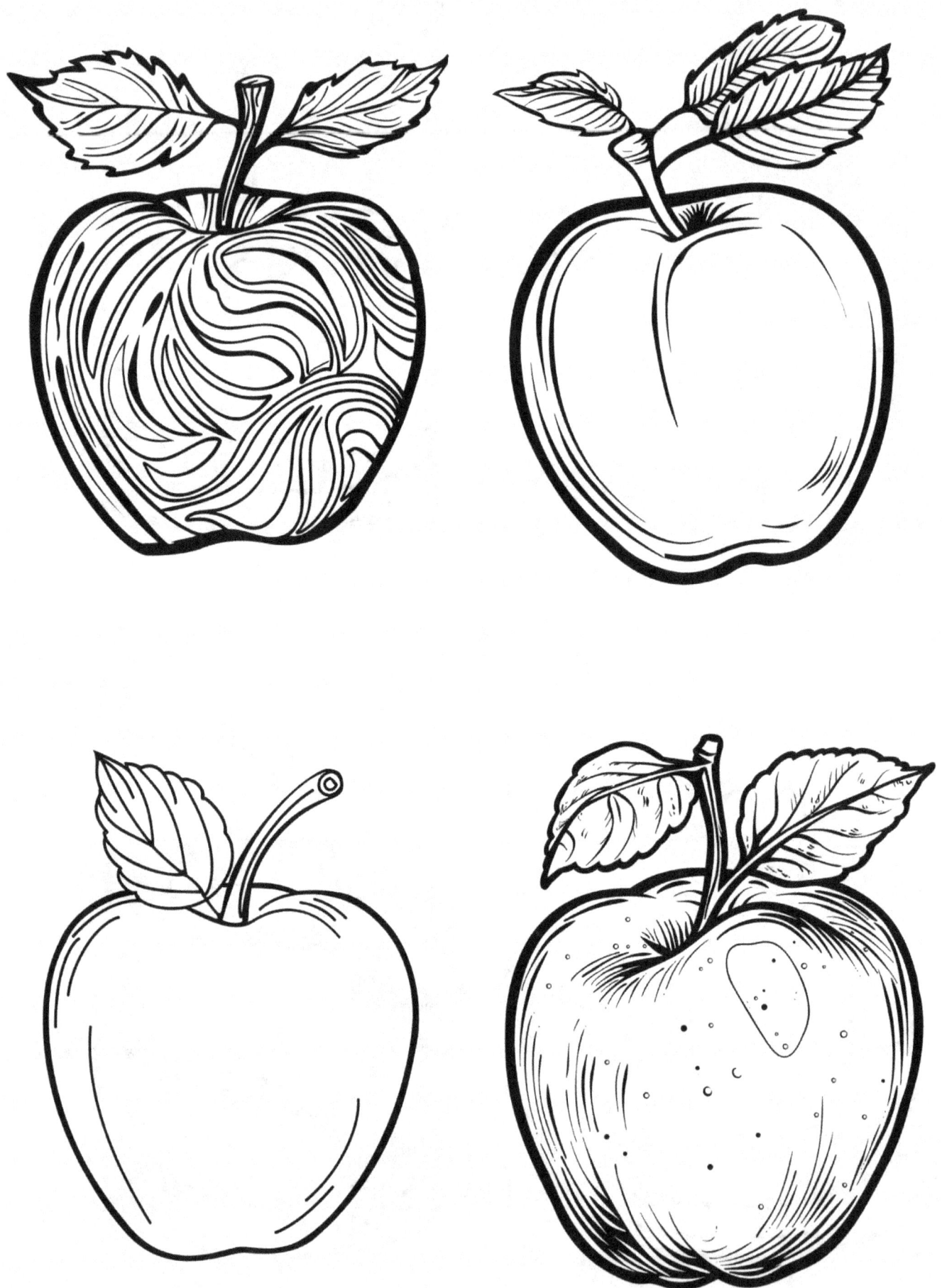

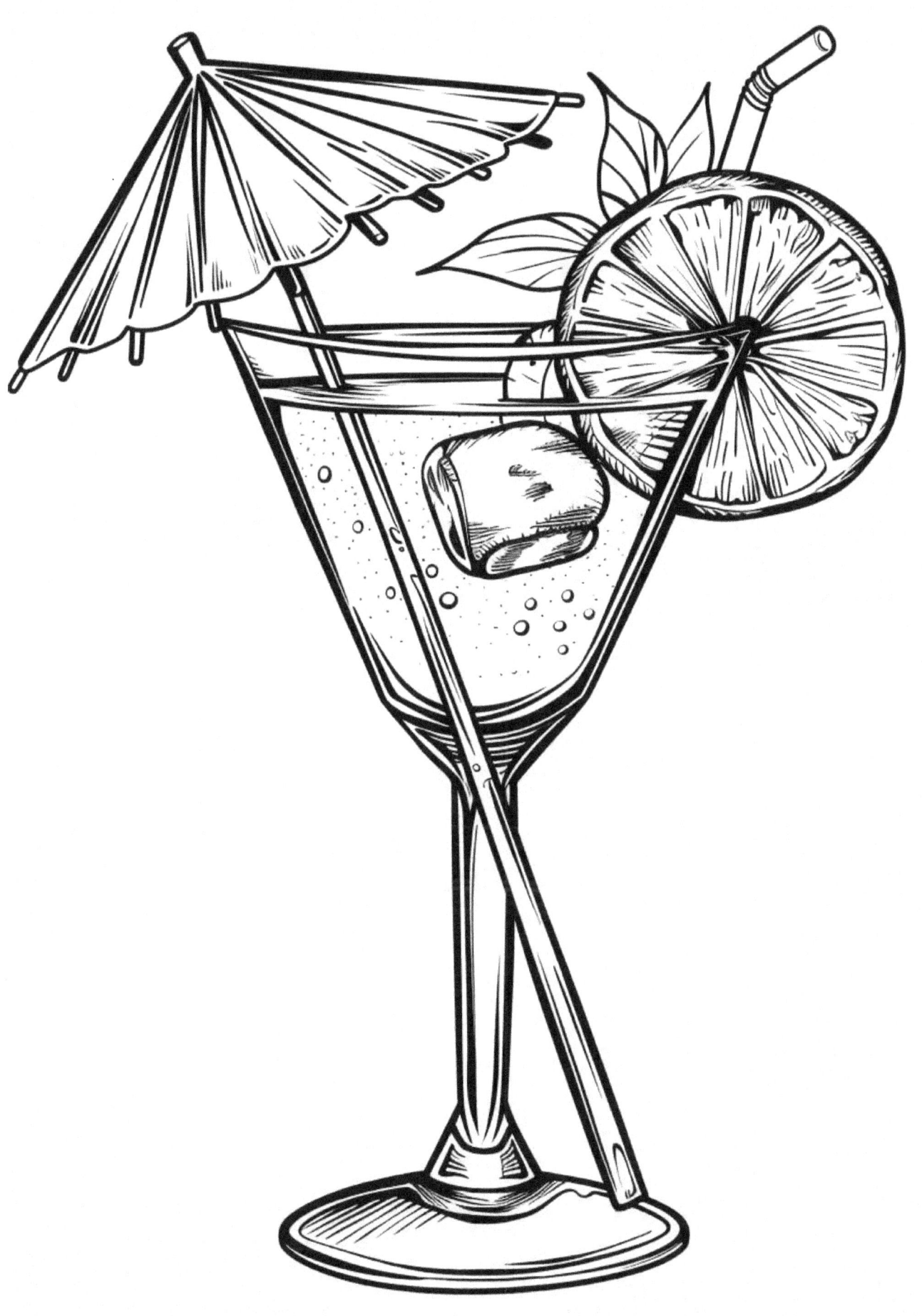

www.ingramcontent.com/pod-product-compliance
Lightning Source LLC
Chambersburg PA
CBHW082336220526
45470CB00008B/2529